Early Praise for *Competing with Unicorns*

If you're a leader who'd like more insight into the real world of tech unicorns like Spotify, if you'd like to understand how they go about impacting the world, this is the book for you. Packed with insights from various unicorns, Jonathan Rasmusson gives us the truth behind the mythology.

➤ **Diana Larsen**
Co-founder & Chief Connector, Agile Fluency Project LLC

In *Competing with Unicorns* you are invited behind the curtain of Spotify (and to peek in on other tech unicorns too) to see what happens there, guided by a long-time agile coach and developer in the company, written with Jonathan's patented humorous and easy-going style. I recommend this book to anyone that wants to be inspired, see beyond the practices, and understand what it takes to make a unicorn dance and succeed.

➤ **Marcus Hammarberg**
Head of Curriculum, Salt

A great book for companies that are going through a digital transformation, especially in software, and for smaller startups that are going through scaling challenges on how to organize and structure themselves in a way that gets them to "think strategic, but act local."

➤ **Luu Duong**
VP Software Development, eCompliance

Jonathan shares his experiences with Spotify to help you understand how their culture and the way they work can help traditional organizations adapt and take advantage of what they have learned through trial and error.

➤ **Janet Gregory**
Agile Testing Coach, Dragon Fire Inc.

Competing with Unicorns

How the World's Best Companies Ship Software
and Work Differently

Jonathan Rasmusson

The Pragmatic Bookshelf

Raleigh, North Carolina

Many of the designations used by manufacturers and sellers to distinguish their products are claimed as trademarks. Where those designations appear in this book, and The Pragmatic Programmers, LLC was aware of a trademark claim, the designations have been printed in initial capital letters or in all capitals. The Pragmatic Starter Kit, The Pragmatic Programmer, Pragmatic Programming, Pragmatic Bookshelf, PragProg and the linking *g* device are trademarks of The Pragmatic Programmers, LLC.

Every precaution was taken in the preparation of this book. However, the publisher assumes no responsibility for errors or omissions, or for damages that may result from the use of information (including program listings) contained herein.

Our Pragmatic books, screencasts, and audio books can help you and your team create better software and have more fun. Visit us at *https://pragprog.com*.

The team that produced this book includes:

Publisher: Andy Hunt
VP of Operations: Janet Furlow
Executive Editor: Dave Rankin
Development Editor: Michael Swaine
Copy Editor: Sakhi MacMillan
Indexing: Potomac Indexing, LLC
Layout: Gilson Graphics

For sales, volume licensing, and support, please contact *support@pragprog.com*.

For international rights, please contact *rights@pragprog.com*.

ISBN-13: 978-1-68050-723-2
Book version: P1.0—March 2020

Contents

Acknowledgments

There are a lot of people to thank for making a book like this happen. Andy Hunt for creating a wonderful company for aspiring authors, and Michael Swaine for all the wonderful edits. All the reviewers: Marcus Hammarberg, Lisa Crispin, Janet Gregory, Gary Bergmann, Kristian Lindwall, Diana Larsen, Luu Duong, Aleksandr Kudashkin, and David W. Robinson whose feedback made this book better. My lovely wife Tannis whose help and support enable me to write. And to all the great people at Spotify who showed me a better way of working. Specifically my managers Marcus Frödin and Kristian Lindwall for continuously challenging me to reach higher and go further.

Thank you Mom and Dad for all your love and support.

It's Good to See You

Today's tech unicorns develop software differently. They don't do textbook agile. They certainly don't do Scrum. What they do do is something completely different. Something that enables them to scale like an enterprise while working like a startup.

This book is about taking you behind the scenes, and showing you how the Googles, Facebooks, Amazons, and Spotifys of the world do it.

- How they scale
- How they organize
- How they empower
- And how they trust

In essence how they work.

This will not only help you and your teams work better. It will give you insight into how these companies move so fast, innovate so quickly, and what the rest of us need to do to compete and keep up.

How to Read This Book

While you are of course free to jump to any section of the book at any time, there is some method to the madness.

The first chapter of the book explains what the world of software delivery looks like through the eyes of a startup and what traditional companies need to rediscover to compete in the future on product.

The middle chapters of the book will give you a sense of what working at one of these tech companies feels like and some of the profound differences in how tech companies are led, organized, and aligned versus more traditional ones.

The last part of the book then dives into culture and explains the cultural differences between how unicorns work versus the rest of us in more traditional companies. Turns out we all value the same things—unicorns just value them differently.

Definitions and Language

Throughout the book I use several terms loosely, which I will attempt to put some context and clarification round.

Startup

When I say startup, know that I am referring to a small company, numbering no more than fifty people, armed with little more than an idea or insight, and looking to take on the world through an innovative product or service.

Tech Companies and Unicorns

Unicorns are those magical, extremely rare tech companies, who have really made it. These are the Googles, Amazons, Facebooks, and Spotifys of the world. When you hear unicorn, think billion-dollar company that still operates like a startup. When you hear tech company, think wannabe unicorn that hasn't yet made it. For the purposes of this book, I use these terms interchangeably, and you can think of them as one and the same.

Also, while many of the unicorns work and collaborate in similar ways, most of the examples we're going to cover will come from my experiences as an agile coach and engineer at Spotify. So while we'll occasionally cover Google, Apple, Facebook, and Amazon, the bulk of the material will come from the former.

Enterprise and Traditional Companies

These are the big, lumbering, slow to change companies we work at day-to-day and know and love. These are going to be the companies against whom we're going to contrast unicorns, because these are the companies that stand to improve the most.

Ready Player One?

You can't take this stuff too seriously, and it helps if you approach the material with a bit of a sense of humor.

To that end, I have lightened things up with pictures, war stories, and other knickknacks to make the material more appealing along the way.

If you see a bit of fruit, know you are about to receive an unbelievably insightful pearl of wisdom as shown in the first figure on page xiii.

SMALL EMPOWERED CROSS-FUNCTIONAL TEAMS ARE THE FOUNDATION OF FAST-PACED PRODUCT DEVELOPMENT AND INNOVATION.

And when you see the gorilla, take a minute to reflect on something you just read and think about how it might affect you and your organization.

 # FOOD FOR THOUGHT

The top three things keeping my team from feeling completely empowered are:

1. _____

2. _____

3. _____

⬅— *Write here* ✏️

Let's begin.

CHAPTER 1

What's Different About Startups

Startups iterate, are super-focused on product, and put a premium on learning. Ask any traditional company if they value these things and they'll undoubtedly say: "Yes. Of course we do!" But if you watch their actions, you'll see they don't.

In this chapter we're going to see what makes startups different, what traditional companies need to rediscover if they want to compete on product, and why both view the purpose of software so differently.

Gaining this insight will not only enable you to see what delivery practices need to change in order to do new product development, it will kick-start the cultural and attitude changes necessary to start working this way.

Startups Are from Mars

When you first join a startup (or a unicorn that still operates like one), you immediately feel a difference. No longer is software development about time, dates, and budgets. Now it's all about the customer, impact, and learning.

To see why, let's quickly look at why startups don't value the things we do in the enterprise (things like conformance to plan) and instead put so much emphasis on exploration, discovery, and learning.

Existence Not Guaranteed

Startups are living on borrowed time. They don't have the luxury of recurring customers or revenue. There's only so much money in the bank. So they need to demonstrate traction and value quickly.

The point here isn't that there is a sense of urgency. Startups always feel the need to move fast. It's that they don't yet know what they need to build—and that they need to figure that out quickly as shown in the figure on page 2.

CONTINUE ?

PRESS START

Live and Die by the Strength of Their Product

In the early days, startups may be able to get by purely on the basis of their idea. But as soon as they take money, they need to demonstrate value fast. Most often this is done through their product.

Product is everything to a startup. It's how they demo. It's how they attract new customers. It's how they raise money. It's how they learn. If the user goes to press play and the music doesn't stream—that's bad.

So product is everything to a startup. And as they experiment, iterate, and learn, they continuously get closer to their product market fit.

Are Searching for Product Market Fit

Product market fit is about finding the perfect product for the right market. This is what startups are continuously searching for because once they find it, they know they've got a winner.

You know you have perfect product market fit when:

- You can't make your product fast enough.
- Usage is growing faster than your ability to add servers.
- Money starts pouring in faster than you can spend it.
- You can't hire fast enough to keep up with demand.

Face a Lot of Unknowns

At the end of the day, startups face a lot of unknowns when trying to find their way in the world. They don't know who their customers are, what their product needs to do, much less how they're going to make money as shown in the figure on page 3.

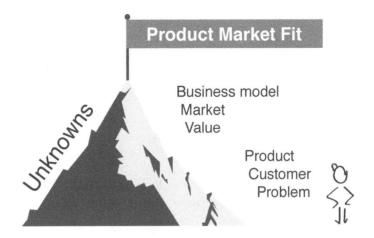

But this is OK. It's all part of the game. A consequence, however, is it tilts startups heavily into experimentation and learning. Because at their heart, startups are really learning machines.

The Learning Machine

Startups care a lot about speed. But something they care about even more is learning.

Startups are trying to outlearn the competition. If they have a great idea, chances are others will think it's a great idea too. So they're in a race. Not a race just in terms of speed. They're in a race about answering unknowns.

This causes them to do certain things. Chief among them when developing software and building product is iterating.

Startups Iterate

Startups iterate relentlessly when building product. Instead of building a product once and declaring victory, they instrument, analyze, and test and then take that knowledge and feed it back into the product over and over again as shown in the figure on page 4.

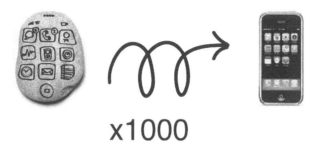

This takes an exploratory and discovery kind of mindset. You're never really done with product. You only get incrementally closer to where you want to be.

This enables them to demonstrate value. Show traction. And ultimately calibrate to something really close to what their customers want.

To do this at scale, however, they need everyone thinking critically. So one thing they do, that we in the enterprise don't, is empower.

Startups Empower

Spotify, Amazon, Google, and Facebook empower and trust people in ways most traditional companies wouldn't dare. They show them financials. They entrust them with all the data. They give developers admin access to their machines. And they are constantly asking their teams: "What can we do to help make you go faster."

It's a liberating way of work, because now instead of blaming management for a bad schedule, or crappy computers or environments, the teams are responsible for all these things themselves.

Unicorns out-trust and -empower teams when compared to traditional companies. And it shows in the quality of the work, and the quality of the product.

So the purpose of software delivery for startups is to:

- Experiment and learn
- Calibrate toward product market fit
- Demonstrate value to investors
- Prove to themselves they're on the right track

So let's now switch gears and see what the purpose of software development looks like through the eyes of the big traditional enterprise.

Enterprises Are from Venus

To understand why startups approach software delivery differently than traditional enterprises, you need to understand the different worlds each is coming from.

Startups, and tech companies, live and die by their ability to build product and serve customers. Building product means validating unknowns, getting product in front of customers, and then iterating on it twenty-seven times until they get it right. Highly iterative. Very exploratory. Outward facing.

Enterprises, on the other hand, are more inward facing. Here the focus is more on automating in-house systems all in the name of productivity and efficiency. With known requirements, in-house customers, and relatively few unknowns, the focus here is more around managing expectations, predictability, and planning.

What's changing for enterprises is that these two worlds of product and in-house enterprise development are now colliding. As startups continue to enter and disrupt traditional markets, enterprises are having to respond with new products and services at a speed and pace they're not used to. And here the startups have a real advantage.

With their focus on the customer, ability to identify gaps in markets, and aptitude to quickly adapt and learn, startups leave enterprises in the dust when it comes to execution. And what enterprises are quickly learning is that the enterprise software playbook they use to ship in-house software doesn't work when it comes to building product. It's the wrong vehicle for the job.

Which is why when enterprises do try to compete on product, they typically make two big mistakes.

1. TREAT PRODUCT DEVELOPMENT THE SAME AS ENTERPRISE DEVELOPMENT.

2. DON'T GIVE TEAMS ENOUGH AUTONOMY AND TRUST.

Because at their heart, most enterprise companies today aren't learning machines. What they are really into is meeting expectations instead.

Every Company Is Now a Software Company

Mark Andreessen once famously said software is eating the world, and he was right. Apple is becoming a bank. Uber, Airbnb, and Netflix have forever changed the world of transportation, accommodation, and entertainment, and Spotify completely disrupted music. And at the heart of it all is software.

As Microsoft CEO Satya Nadella put it: "Every company is now a software company." And whether you make cars, sell insurance, or run a bank, software is at the heart of it. And your company's ability to wield and create it will only continue to play a bigger role in your company's success.

Which is why just about every car manufacturer in the world now has an office in Silicon Valley. Not because Silicon Valley knows anything about cars. More because it knows a lot about software and how to create it.

www.satellitetoday.com/innovation/2019/02/26/microsoft-ceo-every-company-is-now-a-software-company/

The Expectation-Setting Machine

Ask any enterprise if they value learning, and the answer should be a resounding yes. But if you watch their actions, you'll see they value something even more—meeting expectations.

It starts at the top, with the CEO who begins by setting expectations about the upcoming year and what shareholders can expect from the company in the next quarter.

These expectations then get translated into annual budgets and eventually trickle down to teams in the form of projects and plans.

These projects and plans then become hard commitments. To ensure these expectations are met, enterprises then hire cadres of professionals called project managers who shepherd these commitments through the organization and spend a lot of time and energy ensuring everything goes according to plan. Tracking, reporting, and conformance to plan are rewarded above all else. And from a software delivery point of view, this is what success in the enterprise looks like.

When you compare these two worlds, the differences between how startups and enterprises approach delivery becomes much clearer as shown in the table on page 7.

Enterprise	Startup
Inward facing	Outward facing
Following plans	Learning
Automating existing systems	Creating new product
Few unknowns	Many unknowns
Project driven	Product driven
One shot	Iterative
Date & budget	Customer & impact
Top down	Bottom up
Low empowerment & trust	High empowerment & trust
Stick to the plan	Create the plan

Enterprise software delivery is largely an inwardly facing exercise in system automation. The customer is known. The requirements are known. And even if there are details to be worked out, there's an existing system the team can study to figure out what to automate. Discovery isn't valued here. Sticking to the plan is.

Startups are the complete opposite. Startups are looking for the plan. They're trying to discover what their customers want. There's no one sitting down the hall telling them what to build. Startups need to engage real customers and discover it—which is why startups put such a premium on learning, and why delivery takes a much more exploratory and iterative approach.

SO WHICH IS BETTER?
THE STARTUP APPROACH
OR THE ENTERPRISE APPROACH?

It's not a matter of which is better—they solve two completely different sets of problems.

The enterprise approach is good for planning and predictability. Companies can plan a year in advance, spec out what they would like to build, and then treat those projects as one-off initiatives. Highly predictable. Great for upfront planning.

The startup product development cycle, however, is different. Here the product can't be treated as a one-off. It simply needs to be done. And the path to getting there isn't a straight line. It's highly iterative. This requires ongoing investment, a longer time horizon, and a much greater emphasis put on discovery and learning—a very different approach and attitude toward delivery.

And this is where enterprises who are trying to stay nimble and compete struggle. Enterprises need to see software delivery not purely as a means of automating existing in-house systems but as a tool of discovery that can lead to new products, services, and capabilities never before imagined. It just requires a different way of thinking.

Ironically, all big slow-moving enterprises were once small nimble startups themselves. They've just forgotten how to flex that muscle that made them successful in the first place.

And this is really what makes these unicorns successful. They've found a way to let most of their teams operate like mini-startups, while gaining all the economies of scale that come with being an enterprise.

Build It and They Will Not Come

I once worked as a project manager for a company that wanted to pivot into a completely new vertical of work. Instead of selling electricity and power (which they were very good at), they wanted to get into the cattle industry (how hard could it be?). Turns out it was pretty hard.

Instead of building a cheap prototype, shipping something quick, and seeing if anyone would show up, they treated this new venture like any other in-house software project. They set aside a couple million dollars, spent two years building the thing, only to ship it and discover no one actually wanted it. Complete failure. CEO was fired.

The point of this story is that enterprises wanting to act and innovate like startups can't use the same playbook for in-house software development. It's a completely different game, with a completely different set of rules, and you need to unlearn what made you successful in the enterprises (following plans) and instead adopt a much more exploratory mindset.

You can't just build it and expect them to come. And many a startup has fallen prey to this line of thinking.

What This Means for You

Here's the takeaway for you: if you want to create teams that are capable of building great product, you need to change the lens through which they see the world. That means the following:

1. Redefine success

Success is no longer about conforming to plan. Success for us in product development is discovery and learning—which is why you are going to see your first product come out very fast. And then another and another quickly after that. There will be missteps. But with each release the product will get better. And we will know because we'll be looking for traction and measuring impact and value every step of the way.

2. Adopt a learning mindset

This means starting with questions, instead of going in assuming you have all the answers. You may have a hunch around what a great product might look like. But until you validate it, you don't really know. So you're going to want to focus a lot more on experimentation and learning, and not assume you've got everything figured out.

3. Find people who are comfortable dealing with unknowns

Working this way means going out there and finding answers—not sitting back and waiting for someone to hand the spec to you. No one is going to give you the requirements. You need to go out there and discover them for yourself. This makes some people uncomfortable. And many would rather just sit back and be told what to do. These are the wrong people for this type of work. You aren't looking for settlers here. What you need are explorers and pioneers.

4. Remove any stigma around failure

Failure is part of the game when building product. And if your company punishes failure, you're going to have a hard time recruiting the very people you need. So remove the stigma around failure. Let your team and the company know that we expect to fail a few times before getting things right—and that this isn't a one shot deal. The first release is just the beginning.

5. Empower and trust them to get the job done

This sounds like a cliche, but most companies don't really trust their employees (at least the way tech companies do). Great product is built by highly empowered and trusted teams. And in Chapter 3, Empower Through Squads, on page 23, you're going to learn how to empower your teams while supporting them organizationally along the way.

Look. I don't want to make any of this sound easy. You're going to face resistance from all sorts of angles in your organization. You are redefining success. Changing career paths. And moving the goal line on what it means to be successful and get promoted. Changing the status quo is never easy, and you may well run into people who will fight this tooth and nail every step of the way.

 # Warning: Not everyone likes working this way

But the good news is that things are changing. As traditional companies continue to be challenged and disrupted, more and more are realizing they don't really have a choice. To survive they need to get better at building new products. They know they need to level up. And to do that, they're going to have to get out there and rediscover the very things that made them successful when they were small upcoming startups themselves.

The first step is changing perspective—which you just completed. The next step is changing how we organize and do the actual work—which is the focus of the next chapter.

Getting Away from the Mothership—How the IBM PC Got Built

Changing mindsets isn't a problem only non-tech companies face. IBM went through this when transitioning from an area of dominance, mainframe computing in the 1970s, into an area where it had little to no experience—the personal computer.

Realizing they were losing market share in the minicomputer space to the likes of DEC and Wang, IBM was determined not to be left behind in personal computers. There was just one problem.

No product ever shipped at IBM without taking 300 people three years to develop. IBM didn't have time for the old playbook. They needed something new now.

That's when Bill Lowe stepped up and said he could do it in a year, with a much smaller team, on one condition. They leave the mothership, IBM corporate promise to leave them alone, and they get complete control and say in how they build the product. IBM agreed.

They let the PC team set up in far away Boca Raton, Florida. They let the team decide how to source parts, how to allow third-party vendors to contribute software, and basically act as a completely independent business unit. And in one year, with an operating system provided from a then-budding new startup called Microsoft, the IBM PC was built, delivered ahead of schedule, in twelve months—a time faster than any other hardware product in IBM's history. And a new wave in personal computing had begun.

www.ibm.com/ibm/history/exhibits/pc25/pc25_birth.html

FOOD FOR THOUGHT

What would your software delivery process look like
if you didn't have projects?

_____

_____

	A little	A lot
How much leeway do your teams have in product they build?	☐	☐

	Often	Sometimes	Never
How often do your teams go back and iterate on what they have already built?	☐	☐	☐

	The team	Someone else
Who maintains the software your teams build?	☐	☐

Think Different

Product development is different from enterprise development. Unlike enterprise software development, which optimizes for following a plan, startups and tech companies are learning machines—which means they put a premium on learning, experimentation, and discovery.

To build product this way, you need to start getting comfortable with working in the unknown, having a different definition of success, and removing the stigma of failure when building new product.

With this frame of mind, we're now ready to go deeper and see why unicorns don't use the number one instrument we do in the enterprise for getting things done—the project—and instead use something that gives a lot more power and autonomy to teams. Something called a mission.

CHAPTER 2

Give Purpose with Missions

Tech companies don't do projects. They do missions instead. And in this chapter you're going to learn why. Learning how to define work in terms of missions will not only give your teams purpose and encourage them to find their own answers. It will put the responsibility and accountability for fulfilling the mission where it belongs—with them.

By the end of this chapter you'll know what missions are, why they're a better vehicle for building product, and how they enable tech companies to move so fast.

The Problem with Projects

Projects are great when you need to plan out a year in advance what next year's work is going to look like, but they're a lousy way for building anything new. For one thing, they are too short-term.

Projects, by their very definition, have a beginning and an end. And when the project is over—that's it. Everyone packs up and goes home. Product development, however, doesn't work like that. In product development, the first version of your product isn't the end. It's the beginning—which leads to the next thing projects aren't particularly good at. Iterating.

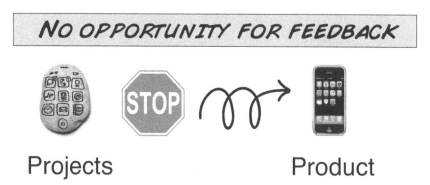

Product development is a highly iterative process. You build one version. Ship it. Get feedback. And repeat twenty-seven times. Projects aren't built for that. With projects you ship the first version. Declare victory and call it a day. They aren't built for acting on feedback or applying learnings.

Projects are also too rigid. When given a project, the goalposts have been set, the path forward is clear, and you don't have a lot of room to deviate or take advantage of new insight, regardless of what you discover along the way. If it's not part of the plan, we don't do it.

But even more frustrating is how disempowering projects are. They encourage you not to think.

Not being able to follow through on your instincts and not being able to incorporate your learnings in the name of time and budget make teams not think or care—which is exactly the opposite of what we need when building product.

And that's really what it comes down to—projects just focus on the wrong things.

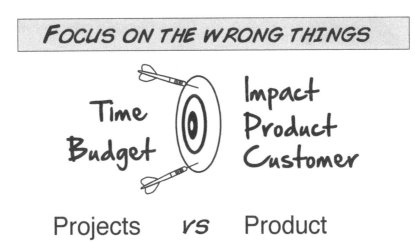

At a tech company, no one cares if your project is +/-10%. That question doesn't even make sense. What does make sense is proof, and that we are building something our customers want, and that we are heading in the right direction toward something valuable.

For these reasons tech companies don't use projects. They simply don't work. What they use is something else. Something that:

- Gives teams an incentive to think longer-term
- Gives teams the time and space to explore
- Lets them incorporate learnings as they go
- Puts the focus back on the work
- Values impact over conformance to plan

Enter the Mission

Missions are high-level goals, given to teams, to direct them in their work toward fulfilling the company's greater purpose.

Google, for example, has a North Star goal of organizing the world's information. That's their purpose. Missions in aid of that would be making search fast, making search accurate, and making all the world's information easy to find.

Tech companies use missions instead of projects to define work. For example, at Spotify we had missions like these:

- Make discovering new music easy
- Win the living room
- Own the morning commute

But missions don't just have to be about product. They can be about non-product things as well:

- Enable other engineering teams to go faster
- Make setting up cloud storage easy
- Prepare the company for the upcoming IPO

In other industries, missions could be something like these:

Industry	Example Missions
Cable company	Win connectivity in the home
Banks	Own casual payments
Financial technology	Detect fraud instantly

The advantages of defining work in terms of missions, instead of projects, are numerous.

Missions Engage the Team

Instead of using people for their backs, missions engage people for their brains. As we will see in the next chapter on squads, Chapter 3, Empower Through Squads, on page 23, the people doing the mission are the ones creating the work. This engages the team, gets them thinking about the solution, and lets them drive the work.

Missions Give People a Sense of Purpose

Purpose is huge. When you come into work knowing that what you do today is going to make someone's life easier, that puts wind in your sails and makes work meaningful. It makes you want to come in. Do your best work. And look forward to doing it all over again tomorrow and the next day after that.

Missions Better Align Incentives

Because teams know they are in it for the long haul, and they are the ones who are going to be iterating and maintaining what they build, they put more care and attention into their work. Which is one of the big reasons why tech company product is of higher quality. It's because the people building the systems are the ones who are maintaining it. That's big.

Not only does it result in better product, it leverages the collective experience and wisdom people develop over time. Instead of disbanding the team at the end of a project, teams on missions stay together.

Finally, missions put the focus back on what really matters. The work. Not the budget and the schedule, which in and of themselves offer no value.

You can sum up the differences between projects and missions like this:

Projects	Missions
Have a budget	The team is the budget
Have an end	Go on indefinitely
Short term	Long term
Have project managers	Have no project managers
Hand off work	Maintain what they build
Disband upon completion	Stay together
Focus on the plan	Focus on the customer
Values meeting expectations	Values impact
Driven from the top down	Driven from the bottom up

For motivated teams with purpose, projects are of no value—which is why tech companies don't use them. Instead they give teams purpose, focus on the one thing that does matter, the work, and remove all distractions getting in the way—which is a big reason why they move so fast.

Maybe That's Why We Did Things So Fast

Startups aren't the first to toss projects to the side. Big companies do this, too, when they need to move fast. In 1952 IBM needed a new business computer quickly. So instead of meticulously planning everything out, they threw aside the budgets and schedules and let the team manage the work themselves.

"Maybe that's why we did things so fast. We didn't have schedules to slow us down." Jerrier Haddad, managing engineer on the IBM 701.

Source: https://www.ibm.com/ibm/history/ibm100/us/en/icons/ibm700series/

HOLD ON. THERE IS SOMETHING I DON'T GET. HOW CAN A TEAM OPERATE WITHOUT A BUDGET?

When it comes to missions, the budget of the mission is the headcount of the team. That's the budget. So instead of tracking countless little budgets, when it comes to spending, all tech companies track is the headcount of the team.

This is very different from how most companies do budgeting, where you propose a project a year in advance, see if that gets approved in next year's budget, and then have that trickle back down to you the following year. Tech companies don't budget like that. They see it as a complete waste of time.

Instead, they fix the spending for the year, work with the headcount they've got, and do as much as they can with the resources given.

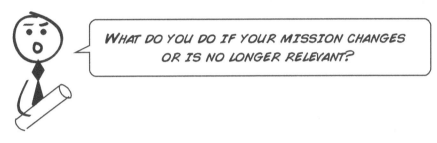

WHAT DO YOU DO IF YOUR MISSION CHANGES OR IS NO LONGER RELEVANT?

Missions periodically do change, and some are shorter-term in nature than others (for example, get the company ready for an IPO). But, generally, missions shouldn't be flippant or small. They should be big, core to your company, and have a purpose.

For example, a mission for a cable company wouldn't be "make installing cable modems in the home easier." That would be something they would do in aid of something bigger like "win connectivity in the home."

Example Mission

Here's an example mission for a team responsible for making listening to music in the car easier.

Squad   Delorean

Mission   Make listening to music in the car the best experience ever

How   By winning the morning commute
Supporting all major car manufacturers
Integrating with two leading platforms
(Apple CarPlay and Android Auto)

Backlog   Fix BMW integration bug
Upgrade Ford support
Feature Flag Tesla
Add analytics for CarPlay

iterate

The team is called Delorean. Their mission is to create the greatest car experience ever. And they are going to do this by integrating their music service into various car manufacturers, thinking really hard about things like the ultimate morning commute, and supporting the two biggest car integrations out there (Apple CarPlay and Google Auto) by ensuring their music runs on those services.

In the next chapter, Chapter 3, Empower Through Squads, on page 23, we'll get into what a squad is and how it is different from your typical enterprise agile team, but for now, note the following:

1. There is no project

The Delorean team has no project. There's no budget (in the traditional sense). And there's no project manager. The team works with their product owner, who is plugged into the overall product strategy of the company and, together, they come up with the priorities and backlog on how best to meet the mission given to the team by leadership.

2. Continuously iterating

The team is never really done. The mission is a destination—one they can never quite reach but are striving to get to. This is a major shift in attitude and thinking.

Instead of doing a series of stories once and declaring victory, the team is continuously revisiting past work and looking for better ways to improve the experience.

That means periodically doing the same story multiple times, each time collecting more data, through which comes better insight—and then ultimately triangulating toward a better solution. All things enterprises typically don't do when executing through a project.

3. The team owns the backlog

This is a subtle but important point—while leadership sets the mission, the team gets to decide how to get there. And one of the instruments they use for showing how they intend to do that is the backlog.

The team creates their own work. They decide what needs to be built. And together with the product owner they create the stories for the backlog. This is a complete 180 reversal from project-based work, where the stories are already defined and handed to the team so they can simply chop the vegetables.

When giving a team a mission:

- Make it important to the company.
- Make it something they can own (with few dependencies on others).
- Work with them to come up with a plan on how to get there.

Does your team have a mission? _____

If so, do they know what it is? _____

Does a mission play a significant role
in guiding your team's work? _____

Are people taking a long- or short-term view
toward the work they are doing? _____

Give Purpose

Projects are the wrong vehicle for building new product. They lack the flexibility and feedback mechanisms necessary for product development—which is why unicorns and other leading tech companies don't use them.

What they use instead are missions—long-term goals teams can take complete ownership of and really figure out and own. By arming teams with missions, people become more engaged, do higher-quality work, and are given the time and space necessary to discover what is really needed.

In the next chapter on squads, Chapter 3, Empower Through Squads, on page 23, we're going to see how teams take their missions and act on them. We'll then see how mission-led squads set their own expectations, come up with their own plans, and create their own work. Get ready to enter the world of the squad.

Empower Through Squads

In this chapter we're going to look at the engine through which most tech companies build product—small, autonomous, highly empowered teams. Or as they call them at Spotify—Squads.

Learning the mechanics behind the squad will not only enable you to build better, higher-quality product. You'll see how tech companies make better decisions, require fewer handoffs, and simplify the coordination of work with others—ultimately enabling everyone to go faster.

This matters because how tech companies set up their teams plays a big part in their success. And by comparing squads with more traditional agile teams in the enterprise, you'll see just how far these notions of empowerment and trust can be taken.

What Is a Squad?

Squads are small, cross-function, self-organizing teams (usually fewer than eight people) who sit together and take full end-to-end responsibility for the product they build.

Squads

Fully staffed teams that take end-to-end responsibilty for the product they deliver.

✓ Maintain what they build

✓ Create their own work

To say that small autonomous teams play an instrumental role in how these tech companies operate would be an understatement. Small autonomous teams are central to just about everything tech companies do. Whether it's building new product, entering new markets, or preparing for an IPO, small autonomous teams are at the heart of how these tech companies operate. And it comes from the deep rooted belief:

 **SMALL EMPOWERED CROSS-FUNCTIONAL TEAMS ARE THE FOUNDATION OF FAST-PACED PRODUCT DEVELOPMENT AND INNOVATION.**

And it is in these squads that tech companies put their trust. They spend a huge amount of time and energy getting these teams right, and they are the hubs around which the rest of the company operates.

Now on the surface, squads don't look all that different from your typical project-based agile team. Dig a little deeper, however, and you'll see some big differences in terms of expectations and how they work. Let's take a look at what some of those differences are now.

> ### Spotify Engineering Culture
>
> For a really good video on how squads work and Spotify culture in general, watch Henrik Kniberg's Spotify Culture videos. Henrik created two great videos describing how Spotify squads work, how Spotify's engineering culture evolved, and how squads fit into the overall organization.
>
> Check them out by Googling "Spotify Engineering Culture".

What Makes Squads Different?

Where squads differ from your typical enterprise agile team is in the sheer amount of empowerment and trust they are given. Tech companies don't view their teams as mere vegetable choppers. They see them more as key collaborators whom they trust not only with building the product but with solving the customer's problem and creating the very product itself.

Here are a few ways enterprise agile teams and squads differ.

Squads Create Their Own Work

Unlike enterprise-based agile teams who get their work handed to them in the form of projects, squads come up with their own solutions to their customers' problems and create the work themselves as shown in the figure on page 25.

Armed with missions, and fully staffed to get the job done, squads decide what to build and how to build it and create whatever work they feel they need to get there themselves.

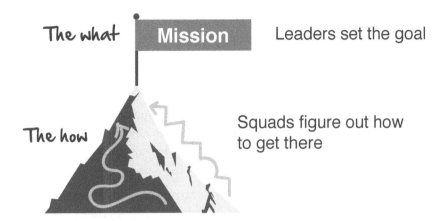

This is a tremendous shift in responsibility. Instead of creating work beforehand, and assuming they have a solution going in (the project-based approach), tech companies give squads missions and ask them to figure it out for themselves. This isn't how most enterprise software delivery works. And it requires a real shift in attitude and thinking.

Squads Maintain What They Build

Squads maintain what they build. Why? Because:

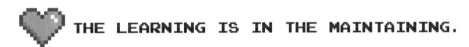

Squads know that the first release isn't the end. It's merely the beginning—and that the real work of figuring out what the customer wants starts after.

This is why squads maintain what they build. Great product takes countless iterations. And the experimentation necessary to figure out how to make the product better can't be handed off to another team. They need to maintain and iterate on the product themselves.

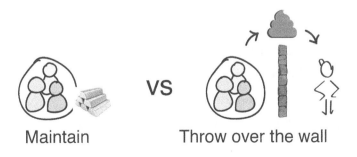

Which is why, unlike project teams that disband at the end of the project and hand their work off to someone else, squads stay together and keep iterating on what they build.

Squads Set Their Own Priorities

Squads get tasked with a lot of things. They build and maintain product. They help other teams out. And periodically they're even asked to put their missions on hold and help push a few other big rocks the company has on the go to drive forward other areas of the company.

Instead of micromanaging squads and continually telling them what to do, tech companies give squads a lot of autonomy and let them set their own priorities. This gives squads the flexibility to know best when to put certain areas of work on hold and when to start other areas up.

That doesn't mean it's a free-for-all. Squads can't just do whatever they want. They need to be good citizens, help other teams out, and align with quarterly goals while maintaining their own products and services.

Which is why the maxim for a squad is:

 BE AUTONOMOUS - BUT DON'T SUBOPTIMIZE.

Which basically means do your work—but not at the expense of others. Review other teams' pull requests (PRs—changes to code), put your work on hold periodically to help other important initiatives, and work for the greater company good—not just what's best for your squad.

Squads Value Impact Over Plans

Squads plan. But plans in themselves aren't the goal. What tech companies value above all is impact—or tangible proof that what you have done has in some way helped the customer.

Impact can be measured in many ways. But usually it's some metric tied to the success of the business.

- How many new sign-ups?

- How many MAU (monthly active users)?

- What's our customer retention?

- Is our NPS score (the likelihood of a customer recommending our product) going up or down?

- How is music consumption trending in the car? On the TV?

- With the recent changes made, can the team now release more quickly into production?

By focusing on key metrics, and worrying less about adherence to estimates, budgets, and plans, tech companies remove a lot of the drama that comes with the traditional project and put all their energy and focus into the work and the customer instead.

Squads Release When Ready

While some squads do have hard deadlines, the majority ship their product when it's ready. You'd think the temptation would be for squads to never ship. But nothing could be further from the truth.

Squads ship regularly and often. And they're always encouraged to build MVPs (minimal viable products) and ship as soon as possible. Why? Because they know the first version isn't going to be right. They want to get that customer feedback. And they can't do that unless they ship. That's why tech companies are always releasing.

But there's a trade-off to all this shipping too. For example, Spotify has a reputation for shipping quality product. And they don't want to ship just anything without first making it look really good.

So it's up to the squad to decide what's good enough and when to ship. This ensures teams have enough time to test. Enough time to debug. And enough time to build it right.

Because unlike enterprise applications that might only serve a handful of people, the product the big tech companies build serve millions—which would lead you to believe that they would be extra careful and paranoid before releasing. But the opposite is true. They release more often, and more regularly than just about every traditional enterprise out there. And a large part of it is because the team ships when they are ready.

Squads Are Highly Autonomous

Because everything isn't hinged around a deadline or a schedule, teams are way freer to experiment, innovate, create, and try out ideas. It's not that all squads aren't deadline driven, or that there's never a schedule to be met. It's just a different attitude toward development.

Instead of merely being machines that take and execute stories, squad members are expected to ask questions, think about what they are doing, and speak up if they don't agree with the direction the team is going:

- Do we need to spike a new prototype for an upcoming integration?

- Should we shift gears and focus on getting ready for the new privacy laws around GDPR?

- Or is this the time to do that major refactoring we've been putting off?

Being autonomous means being able to take a longer-term view, to empower teams to balance the countless trade-offs that come with delivery. This is how tech companies empower and trust.

But not only does all this autonomy lead to better decisions and fewer hand-offs, it's also a more fun, productive way to work. And most people like it when they're given the reins and have a real say in how they work.

Squads Are Staffed Only by People Doing the Work

You don't see a lot of fluff on squads—pretty much everyone there is tied to delivery. Product owners, designers, testers, and engineers all sit together, work iteratively, and ship product.

Two roles you don't see on squads are project manager and Scrum master.

Project managers aren't there, because there's no project. Expectation setting, aligning, and all the other important stuff traditional project managers do still gets done. It's just not tied to the yoke of a project. It's instead driven by the product owner under the umbrella of the mission.

And Scrum masters aren't there because unicorns don't do Scrum.

That's not to say Spotify and others didn't make heavy use of agile coaches early on—they absolutely did. Spotify saw agile coaches as vital for bootstrapping teams in agile delivery, playing a crucial role of cultural ambassador, and stepping in and helping teams work through the inevitable up and downs all teams face when first starting out. Agile coaches played a big role in Spotify's early success and were core team members.

The point here isn't that project managers or Scrum masters aren't important. They absolutely are. For where you work, some of your top people, who can really help you in delivery, may well play either of the roles. So don't shun them when delivering.

Just understand that when push comes to shove, squads are lean, mean delivery machines made up of the people doing the work. So remove anyone who is not directly contributing, and keep the people who are.

Two other roles unicorns rely on heavily that enterprises don't are product manager and data scientist.

Product Managers

Product managers, or PMs (not to be confused with project managers), are the people responsible for guiding the what of the squad. Similar to the Scrum product owner (which is the term we used at Spotify for this role), product managers set the direction the squad heads and are plugged into the overall product and strategy for the rest of the company.

PMs guide the delivery of the product by acting as the source of truth around what the product should do. Working with the team, they define strategy, create roadmaps, come up with feature definitions, and may also be involved in marketing, forecasting, and P&L (profit and loss) responsibilities.

PMs at tech companies:

- Are highly technical (many are former engineers)
- Have good product sense
- Have strong leadership and negotiation skills

They are the drivers who have the ability to see things through to the end.

Which is why they are also highly sought after and valued in tech companies. It's a very important role, one tech companies value greatly (top notch PMs are paid well). And they play a key role in bringing new products and services to life.

The other role you see in tech companies is that of data scientist.

Google's First Product Manager

Marissa Mayer (Google employee number twelve and former CEO of Yahoo) was the first product manager at Google. Realizing there was a need for someone to make product decisions, but who could also speak the language of engineers, Marissa created this new role and went on to define the product manager role and discipline at Google.

Today Google has thousands of product managers building all sorts of product, and today you'll find other tech companies like Facebook and Amazon making great use of product managers too.

Data Scientists

Data scientists are mathematicians and engineers who help teams use data to make product decisions. With the sheer amount of data companies are collecting, there's a need to collect, process, clean, and filter data for decision-making. And because data processing has become so cheap, today everyone can leverage these tools for developing insight—not just senior management.

At Spotify, data scientists would help teams:

- Decide what metrics to collect
- Format and clean data from different formats
- Come up with best practices and naming conventions
- Create hypotheses about what to test
- Determine whether results were statistically significant
- Do data analysis
- Set up reports, summaries, dashboards, and other visualization artifacts

Sometimes this was one person. Sometimes two (it could be a full-time job just getting the data into a state where it could be analyzed). But at Spotify, every squad would have access to someone with this kind of expertise to help collect metrics, use those metrics to make product decisions, and basically gain insight into how their products were being used by customers.

We'll talk more about data scientists and the important role they play at tech companies in Chapter 8, Learn with Data, on page 81.

Two important ingredients for enabling teams to work like squads are to build your products with decoupled architectures, while fostering a culture of empowerment and trust. Let's look at the decoupled architecture first.

Decoupled Architectures

A decoupled architecture is one where various parts of the application have very few dependencies on one another. For example, the very first version of the desktop client Spotify ever built was a big monolith with everything coupled together as shown in the figure on page 31.

Playlists, controls, and recommendation engines were all tightly bound and interwoven. And making changes to one area often had a big effect on the others.

To fix this, Spotify broke the application up into small well-defined parts, with each squad becoming responsible for one respective area in the application. Doing this has several advantages.

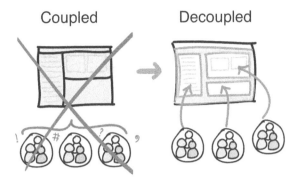

1. Multiple teams can work on the product concurrently

This is how tech companies scale. They take big complicated products and break them down into smaller independent ones. This lets multiple teams work on the product simultaneously and prevents teams from stepping on each other's toes.

2. Decoupled releases

By breaking the app up, teams can also not only work independently, they can release independently. This avoids handoffs, minimizes waiting for other teams to complete their work, and lets squads ship their portion of the product when they're ready.

3. It makes maintenance and debugging way easier

By compartmentalizing functionality, and not spreading it through the product, troubleshooting, debugging, and keeping the product at a high level of quality all become much easier. Some integration bugs will always occur. But this makes tracking them down and fixing them easier.

4. Limited blast radius

When something goes wrong, it doesn't bring down the entire app. Only that area where the thing when wrong is affected. The rest of the app can operate just fine.

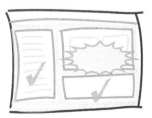

One portion of the app can blow up...

while everything else still works!

So if you want your squads to be independent, you need to find ways to minimize their dependencies on other teams. And if multiple teams are going to work on the same project, one sure way to keep them from stepping all over each other is to decouple your architecture.

Next, let's talk about trust.

Autonomy, Empowerment, and Trust

None of this stuff works without empowerment and trust. If you want teams to make their own decisions, become accountable, and go that extra mile, you need to trust them. It's that simple.

The second you signal that you don't trust a team, or that they're not empowered to solve their own problems, they won't. They'll sit back and wait for you to hand them a project and tell them what to do.

This is perhaps the scariest thing that executives will need to accept when choosing to work this way. Giving teams this much responsibility will initially feel like a big risk.

- What if they don't deliver?
- What if they just sit around all day and build cool stuff?
- What if they never ship?
- It's my butt on the line!

Look—I get it. This can be a scary thing for managers and leaders who are used to hierarchy, are hard-driving, and have had great success in telling others what to do.

All I can tell you is that this is how tech companies work, this is how they scale, and that when you empower and trust your people, you may be surprised by what they can do.

Because you know what? A lot of the people who work at all these great tech companies, building great product, came from traditional companies. They used to work for you!

They're the same rank and file engineers, project managers, testers, and designers that used to work at big traditional companies but were drawn to a different way of working. Empowerment and trust makes people do better work. And if it doesn't, then at least you'll know you've got the wrong people and you can then shift to fixing that. Either way you're ahead.

Tech companies don't simply hire the best people. They make them. And they make them by giving them tough, challenging work, empowering them to do the job, and supporting them when they fail.

People at these companies don't do great work because of free lattes and foosball tables. They excel because they're empowered and trusted.

Tips for Leaders

Here are a couple of quick tips for leaders and managers who want their teams to start working this way.

Let Them Drive

As a leader, you got to where you are because you are smart, hard-working, and are right more often than you're wrong. You can still use all those traits and experience to help your team—just let them drive.

Letting your team drive means not telling them what to do. Give them time and space to figure some things out for themselves. That doesn't mean you can't advise or make suggestions.

But if you start telling them what to do, they aren't going to own it. You will. So avoid the instinct to continually ride in and save the day. Let them drive. Make them own it.

As Steve Jobs once said: "It doesn't make sense to hire smart people and tell them what to do; we hire smart people so they can tell us what to do."

Let Them Make Mistakes

Experience is a great teacher, and making mistakes is a great way to learn. When your team does make mistakes, and they didn't heed your advice, avoid the temptation to say "I told you so." Instead, pick them up off the ground, dust them off, and tell them to try again.

This does two things. One, it signals that it's OK to make mistakes. It's part of the game. Two, it signals that you trust them, and you've got their back.

This way, the next time they do make a mistake, they'll know you're there to support them, and they'll be more open to whatever advice you have to offer.

Be Prepared to Be Wrong

When you do see your team doing something that you think is never going to work, be prepared to be wrong. This has happened to me more times than

I care to admit. Not only was I wrong in my analysis of the problem, the team came up with a much better solution than what I was going to suggest. You'll be pleasantly surprised when the team comes up with their own solution, while learning something yourself at the same time.

Choose a Fun Name

This may not sound like a big deal, but let squads pick their own names. Picking a name establishes that squad's brand. Their identify. What they stand for. In tech companies your squad is like your family. Kind of like the sports team you play for.

It's also how you communicate and project yourself across the company. It's how people figure out what team you're on, what you do, and it's a heck of a lot more fun than saying "I work in finance." Instead, tell them your squad is responsible for making the money flow and that the Iron Bank sent you.

Q&A

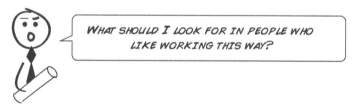

WHAT SHOULD I LOOK FOR IN PEOPLE WHO LIKE WORKING THIS WAY?

Look for people with the following characteristics:

- Independent
- Enjoy being responsible
- Like taking the initiative
- Like controlling their own destiny
- Dislike being micromanaged
- Are into continuous learning
- Are not afraid to fail
- Like collaborating with others
- Are good team players

That may sound like a basket list of things we'd all like to find in teammates. But if you've got people who like to sit back, get projects handed to them, and be told what to do, it's not going to work.

You want people who care. Who aren't in it purely for the money. And just want to do good work because…what's the alternative? And you can absolutely attract those people by simply giving them a lot of empowerment and trust.

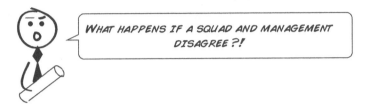

WHAT HAPPENS IF A SQUAD AND MANAGEMENT DISAGREE ?!

Sometimes squads and management don't see eye to eye. For example, I was once working with the team that put Spotify on the Sony Playstation, and this work had a hard deadline. When Sony turned their music service off, we needed to be there. There was no missing the date.

This, of course, led to all sorts of challenges, as you can imagine. And when it became apparent that we weren't going to make the date, management suggested to the squad they either outsource some work to another team or take new team members on. The team said no.

This, of course, put management in a bind. Management thought the team wasn't going to make the deadline. The team thought everything was fine. What do you do?

In this case management backed off a bit, but when crunch time came they offered one of the company's best JavaScript engineers, on loan, for a few short weeks—just to get them over the hump. They agreed. He joined for a week. The team loved him. And decided to let him stay. We made the deadline.

This kind of scenario has no black and white answer, but generally you want the team to make the decision. And when they are empowered, trusted, and asked what would be best for the company (not just themselves), the right things usually happen. But you want them to come to that conclusion themselves.

Because the more you step in, and the more you tell them what to do, the less empowered and trusted they are going to be. Which isn't what you want.

WHO MANAGES THE SQUADS ?

At Spotify we had a group of managers called a POTLAC, who were responsible for the well-being of the team. POTLACs consisted of a chapter lead (we cover this role in Chapter 4, Scale with Tribes, on page 39), an agile coach, and the product owner from the squad. It was this group's job to keep tabs on the health of the team, handle any issues that came up, and make sure they were getting everything they needed to be successful.

Sometimes this meant finding the right mix of people. Other times it meant making introductions to people on behalf of the squad to other parts of the company. But generally speaking, this was an experienced group with the squad's health in mind, and if the squad failed, they failed. So they were very motivated to help the squad get things right.

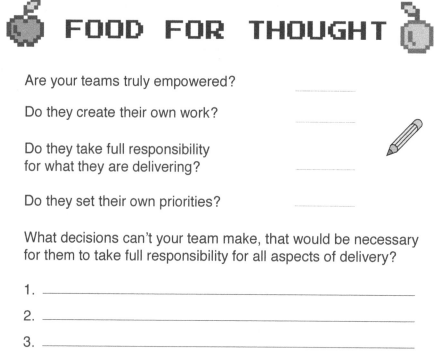

FOOD FOR THOUGHT

Are your teams truly empowered?

Do they create their own work?

Do they take full responsibility
for what they are delivering?

Do they set their own priorities?

What decisions can't your team make, that would be necessary
for them to take full responsibility for all aspects of delivery?

1. _____

2. _____

3. _____

Empower

OK, we covered a lot here, and this is a really important chapter. We now understand that tech companies build product through highly empowered, trusted teams called squads. And by building their products with highly decoupled architectures, they enable a lot of teams to work on the same product at the same time.

It's the company leader's job to set the mission (the what). And it's the squad's job to come up with the solution (or the how).

In the next chapter, Chapter 4, Scale with Tribes, on page 39, we're now going to see how tech companies take these small autonomous teams and apply these philosophies at scale. Turn the page to continue our adventure and dive into the world of tribes, chapters, and guilds.

Scale with Tribes

Small autonomous teams are great, but there's one thing they don't do—scale. How do we take something that works so well in the small and scale it across the whole company? That's what this chapter is about.

By learning how to organize your teams into tribes, chapters, and guilds, you'll learn how to keep that startup feeling of empowerment and trust, while simultaneously contributing to something bigger as a whole.

The Challenge of Scaling

Scaling is tough. It's one of the biggest challenges unicorns face once they find product market fit and need to grow and hire rapidly. Every tech company wants their teams small and nimble—yet at the same time avoid becoming bloated and slow like the very incumbents they're trying to displace.

What these tech companies are looking for is the best of both worlds. A way to organize teams so they stay small and work like startups, but at the same time scale and grow and gain the efficiencies and clout that come with being a big company.

One way Spotify tackled this problem was to break their workforce into what they call Tribes, Chapters, and Guilds. Let's take a look now at the underlying principles of the model, and then see concretely how it works.

Principles of Scaling

Spotify kept certain principles in mind when it came up with its tribe-chapter-guild model of organization as shown in the figure on page 40.

Let's break these down a bit more.

```
         TRIBE PRINCIPLES
  - SQUADS COME FIRST
  - SERVANT-LEADERS
  - MISSIONS MATTER
  - FULL-STACK FOR MISSIONS
  - SIZE IMPORTANT
  - MOBILITY OK INSIDE TRIBES
  TRIBE / CHAPTER / GUILD
```

Squads Come First

Spotify believes that the company with the best teams will win. So it puts a lot of time and energy into setting up their squads. Squads are the creative engines, where products are crafted. Other organizational constructs (tribes, chapters, and guilds) all exist primarily as scaffolding to support and align their squads. Collaboration and contribution to team success is valued more than individual accomplishment. So Spotify sees developing high-performing squads and building an environment to support, hire, and retain great people as the most important work they do.

We Believe in Servant-Leaders

Spotify likes leaders who focus on the growth and well-being of people and teams in their care. They put the needs of others first and help both people and teams develop and reach their full potential. They hold their leaders accountable for the output, effectiveness, and morale of the organization.

Missions Matter

Squads and tribes must have a clear mission with clearly identified customers. They need clear metrics for success, for which they are accountable.

Tribes are Full-Stack for Their Missions

A tribe should have all the skills required to experiment, learn, and execute on its mission. This means experts in engineering, design, and product relevant to the domain of the mission. There must be enough people in a tribe to support its activities—everything from keeping the lights on to forming cross-functional squads capable of owning their missions and swarming problems when necessary.

Tribe Size Is Important

Experience has shown that the ideal tribe size is somewhere between a minimum of 40 and a maximum of around 150 (Dunbar's number).

This maximum exists to ensure the tribe feels like a cohesive community, where people have an opportunity to develop relationships and the trust necessary for teams to perform well. The minimum supports some level of mobility within the tribe and fits the overall organization model.

We Encourage Mobility Inside Tribes

Spotify believes that it should be easy for people to move freely between squads within a tribe. This mobility is important. However, they didn't want total liquidity. They felt it important to preserve domain expertise within each squad, since maintenance is an essential part of a squad's work. So mobility between tribes should still be an option—but by necessity more difficult.

So those were some of the high-level principles that guided the development of the Spotify model. Let's now dive deeper and see how it works.

Tribes, Chapters, and Guilds

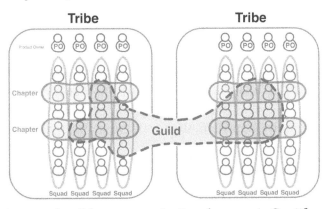

Tribes, chapters, and guilds are organizational concepts Spotify came up with to tackle the problem of scaling. Spotify, like other startups, had to scale fast. That meant figuring out ways of keeping everyone together, while at the same time quickly bring new people on board and making them productive quickly.

That meant experimenting a lot. Spotify tried many different ways of organizing teams, in both traditional and nontraditional ways, before eventually landing on something that enabled their teams to be small and autonomous, while at the same time enabling them to scale and be a part of something bigger.

We'll first take a look at the construct called the tribe, and then see what chapters and guilds do for us beyond that.

Tribes

A tribe is a collection of squads with similar or related missions. Payment, for example, may require several squads to handle sign-in, authorization, and payment for a tech company's services. That would be a tribe. If you had a group of squads who worked on embedding your software into hardware (car, TV, speaker, for example), hardware might be another.

Just like squads, tribes are fully stacked, sit together, and usually number no more than around 150.

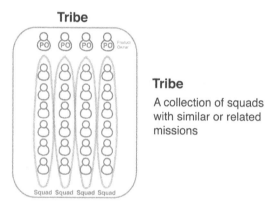

Tribe

Tribe

A collection of squads with similar or related missions

Tribes are like mini-companies within themselves. They take full responsibility for an area of the business, come up with their own plans and goals for making it grow, while simultaneously aligning on really big initiatives called bets (more on that in Chapter 5, Align with Bets, on page 51).

The beauty of the tribe is the synergy you get from having a lot of people working on similar problems together. For example, hardware and speakers might require a similar set of technical challenges faced in TV and car. By grouping these teams together, they can share ideas and code, while moving around freely and readily working with others.

The same principles that hold with squads also hold with tribes—we always want to minimize dependencies.

Just like squads, tribes work best when they aren't dependent on other tribes for work. They can ship when ready. Experience fewer delays. And require fewer handoffs when they aren't waiting for others. So you always want to organize your tribes in a way that minimizes dependencies with others as shown in the figure on page 43.

Try to minimize dependencies between squads & tribes

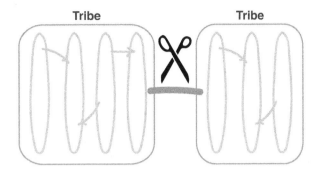

While tribes are great for creating synergy with like-minded squads, we still have a challenge with front-line management. Should an engineer report to a manager for a squad, or someone else in the tribe more closely grouped to their respective discipline? To solve this problem, Spotify created Chapters.

Chapters

A chapter is a group of people within a tribe organized around a particular discipline. For example, all the testers in a tribe would form a QA (quality assurance) chapter. All the web engineers might form another.

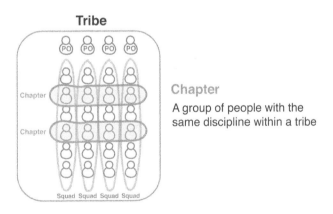

Chapter

A group of people with the same discipline within a tribe

Managing people like this gives engineers the best of both worlds. Day-to-day, they can be part of a highly trusted collaborative team, while at the same time having a front-line manager who understands the nature of their work.

Chapter leads are the managers for the people of a discipline within a tribe. They offer front-line support and handle everything from hiring, salary, career development, and all the other things a typical manager would do.

One difference between a chapter lead and the more traditional line manager at a bigger company is chapter leads still occasionally do real work. Not always day-to-day front-line work (as in delivering a story). But they are still pretty close to the metal and will chip in and offer guidance and advice when needed. Chapter leads are still highly technical.

But the real advantage the chapter brings to the organization is community. By having a group related to a particular discipline, people can meet regularly to discuss new technologies and better practices, while having a forum for sharing news and context within the community.

Tribes and chapters are pretty good are keeping things local, but Spotify found that despite this, there was still a need to communicate and self-organize right across the organization. For that they have guilds.

Guilds

Guilds are groups of like-minded people who are able to span and organize right across the organization.

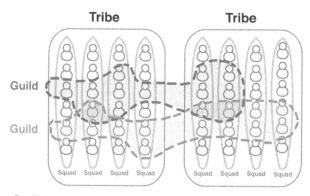

Guild

A group of people within the same discipline
spanning the organization

While not as formal as a chapter, and offering nothing in terms of direct management or support, guilds are a lighter-weight organization structure that anyone can spontaneously create and anyone can join.

The iOS guild, for example, would meet regularly to discuss news and developments in iPhone development. The Android folks would do the same for Android.

The difference between a guild and a chapter is that anyone can join a guild. You don't have to be an iOS developer to attend the iOS guild meetings, and pretty much everyone is welcome.

Guilds are also voluntary. You don't have to go to every guild meeting, though if you did they'd be very happy to see you.

Guilds create their own unconferences—informal get-togethers where people can discuss guild-related issues, help establish best practices, and generally form a company community around that discipline.

But even more than this, guilds give people an avenue to learn and grow. By bringing UX, web developers, and testers together, people can talk about challenges in their craft, level-up by rubbing shoulders with others who are really good at what they do, and generally just get better.

Don't underestimate this. The power of learning, and feeling yourself continuously getting better, is highly attractive to hard-working, smart, intelligent people. It's what keeps your best and brightest sticking around. And forums like guilds give people an opportunity to level-up and grow. And that in itself can be compelling enough for a lot of people to come into work everyday and give it their all.

Another interesting aspect to how tech companies work is the lengths they'll go to keep their people motivated and happy about where in the organization they're working.

Where Would You Like to Work?

All companies periodically go through reorgs, but as tech companies scale, they go through these more often than most.

We didn't do this all the time at Spotify, but during one particularly large reorg, the agile coaches at Spotify facilitated a workshop where the leaders got together and collaborated on the new tribe structure. Only, instead of assigning people to teams within the new tribe, Spotify let the people choose where they would like to work themselves.

Tribe X Re-Organization

What if we let people choose where they'd like to work?

Taking over a large auditorium area for the better part of a week, agile coaches rolled in several whiteboards, listing all the new teams and positions in the new tribes. Then during that week managers met with their direct reports, during one-on-ones, and answered any questions they might have about the new positions and teams in the new world.

What happened next was interesting. Some teams decided to stay together and continue working right where they were. Others formed new teams, grouped with friends, and went looking for new work. Some wanted a change. Others wanted to try completely new jobs.

Initially, not every spot was filled nor every vacancy taken. Nor did everyone get their first choice of team (some backroom negotiating did go on to ensure each team had the necessary composition to get the work done).

But at the end of the day, most people found a spot they more or less liked. Some new teams took less sexy work (so long as they stayed together and worked with friends), while others flexed and went wherever they were needed.

What was remarkable about this exercise was it demonstrated to me how far these tech companies will go to push down decision and encourage people to self-organize. I don't know too many traditional companies who would have let their people choose their teams and sign up for work.

 PUSHING DECISIONS DOWN AS FAR AS YOU CAN ENCOURAGES PEOPLE TO SELF-ORGANIZE.

But tech companies have very fluid organizations. Reorgs like this happen all the time. And what Spotify and other tech companies have found is that people are way more likely to stick around and do better work when they can choose the nature of that work and collaborate with the people they like.

Q&A

WAIT A MINUTE. ISN'T THIS JUST A MATRIX ORGANIZATION?

Yes and no.

You Don't Join a Team When You Join Facebook

When you first join Facebook, you don't join a team. Instead, you work on multiple teams and float for two months. This is by design. Facebook doesn't want you joining a team you don't like.

And this isn't just for new hires. It's for full-timers too. Full-time engineers get to do this for one month every year as a means of exploring other parts of the company and potentially transferring to other teams to pursue other areas of work.

Why would Facebook give their engineers this freedom to move around and try different things out? It's because they know people do their best work when they're working on things they like. And letting them choose maximizes the chances of them coming into work everyday happy and excited.

Remember—teams are everything to these tech companies. And they want to avoid putting you any place that's not right for you or the team you're joining. So if they can avoid putting you somewhere that isn't a great fit, they will.

In a matrix organization similar groups of resources are all pooled together (that is, all the testers would report to a testing manager) and then loaned out to projects where testers are needed. Spotify's matrix doesn't do this. Their matrix is instead tilted much more toward delivery.

By grouping people into stable co-located squads, people of different skill sets collaborate and self-organize to deliver product. That's the vertical dimension of the matrix and is the primary focus since that's how people are physically organized by where they work.

The horizontal part of the matrix, the how, is where knowledge-sharing, tools, and coding practices come in. The job of the chapter lead is to help build their community and grow the discipline.

So in matrix terms the "what" is the vertical dimension and the horizontal the "how." This ensures every squad member knows what needs to be built, while also getting the right support in how to build it.

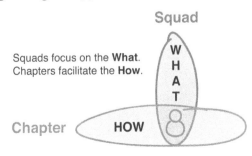

FOOD FOR THOUGHT

What groups should your team regularly be interacting with that they currently are not?

_____

How do people currently level-up, or improve their skills in your organization?

_____

_____

If you had a magic wand, and could suddenly regroup all the teams and departments in your organization, how would you do it?

Draw here

Scale Big but Stay Small

Scaling is hard. Which is why so many startups and tech companies struggle when getting big. But Spotify and others have found ways to keep the speed and autonomy of their small empowered teams, while gaining the benefits of growing into something larger.

- Tribes group squads with related missions.
- Chapters offer front-line discipline support.
- Guilds enable cross-company collaboration.

In the next chapter on bets, you'll see how tech companies align squads around big bets, while simultaneously letting them pursue their own individual missions. Turn the page to learn how to align with bets.

CHAPTER 5

Align with Bets

Small autonomous teams powered by missions are great, but what if you need to do something big. Something that takes multiple teams, working as one, right across the entire company. In this chapter we're going to see how tech companies use company bets to enable cross-company collaboration, ensure the really important stuff gets done first, while still giving teams the latitude and autonomy for day-to-day work.

By the end of this chapter you'll know what company bets are, how they work, and why they are so effective for getting teams working together.

A Thousand Flowers Wilting

In 2014 Spotify had a problem. As it was scaling, it had lots of people working on thousands of little things, but very little of importance was actually getting done. Daniel Ek, Spotify's CEO, had decided to try this thousand-flowers-bloom strategy in the hopes that something good would organically emerge. And a few small things did. But the big stuff—the really important stuff that needed doing was still taking too long—we weren't moving fast enough.

It was obvious that Spotify needed to focus. But how? They didn't want to squash all the great innovation that was going on. And they didn't want to take away any squad autonomy. Yet they needed a way of coordinating massive amounts of work, sometimes requiring multiple teams, in a meaningful, focused way.

This is when Spotify came up with the idea to start focusing organization-wide on just a few things at once—or internally what we like to call "the company bet."

Enter the Company Bet

Company bets are a stack-ranked, prioritized list of the most important things the company would like to get done.

Priortized list of most important things everyone in company should be working on

✓ Forces focus

✓ Ensures most important stuff gets done first

✓ Enables cross-company collaboration

✓ Tool for alignment and prioritization

Aligning with the North Star goal of the company (the very purpose of the company's being), leadership uses these bets to focus the company, communicate priorities, and ensure the most important things are getting worked on first, and everything else second.

Typically, company bets are not small. These are big rocks, requiring the efforts of multiple teams, that will hopefully have a big impact on the business in a relatively short period of time—which is why they get so many resources and attention. At any given time, 30% of the company will be working on a company bet. And these bets provide guidance for what teams should be trying to work on next.

How Do They Work

Every quarter the strategy team gets together and debates what big hairy audacious goals the company should be working on next. Out of these strategy sessions comes a prioritized stack-ranked list, or company bets as shown in the figure on page 53.

STRATEGY TEAM PRIORITIZES BETS EVERY QUARTER

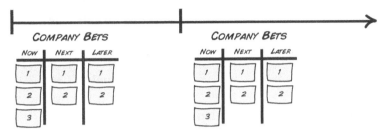

Each bet is accompanied by a two-page brief describing what the bet is, why it's important, and how it will help the company go further.

EACH BET GETS A 2-PAGE BRIEF

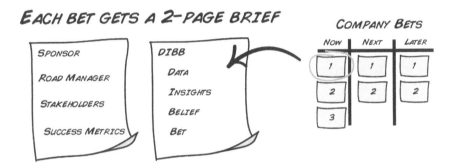

One of these two pages is a DIBB explaining the data and insight that led the strategy team to create that bet in the first place.

DIBBS ARE USED TO DECIDE AND DEBATE

DIBBS is a decision-making framework to formulate tests on the things we think we should do.

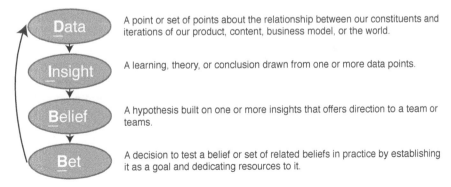

DIBB stands for Data, Insight, Belief, and Bet. At Spotify we used DIBBs as a means to debate and decide how we wanted to invest and win in music. At its heart DIBBs is a decision-making framework that gives people a way to formulate or argue for why they feel their bet is necessary.

For example, in the early years at Spotify, it became apparent that while people were listening to less music on the desktop, mobile consumption was starting to take off. This would have a huge impact on the business, and we weren't ready yet to make that adjustment.

Describing this shift from desktop to mobile in the form of a DIBB made things a lot clearer.

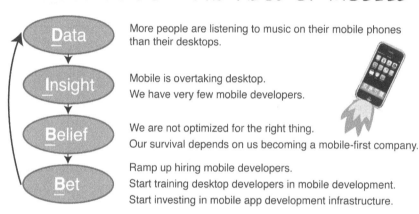

It quickly became apparent what we needed to do. This DIBB became the bet. That pivot into mobile saved the company. And the rest is history.

The Beauty of Working This Way

Lots of advantages come from rallying your company around just a few big bets.

The Important Stuff Gets Done First

Unicorns, like any healthy company, can get easily overwhelmed by the sheer number of things they need to do. Which is why bets are such a good tool for getting the most important stuff done first, saving the least till later as shown in the figure on page 55.

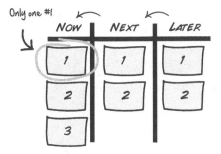

It Enables Fluid Work Force

Bets also enable unicorns to shift company resources a lot more easily when compared to their traditional counterparts. Traditional companies waste a lot of time wrestling with conflicting priorities and misaligned short-term goals, usually resulting in a tremendous lack of coordination and effort.

Bets, on the other hand, give you and your teams a framework for balancing the short-term goals of the team against longer-term goals of the company.

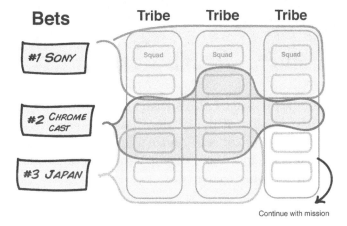

By enabling a team to put their work on hold, and help a company bet out, teams can fluidly move between missions and bets dynamically as they see fit. This leaves the autonomy with the team and lets them decide where they can best spend their time.

It Forces Focus

When you rank your company bet list, you're literally saying: "These are the most important things we need to get done this year. If we can do these things, we're going to have a very good year."

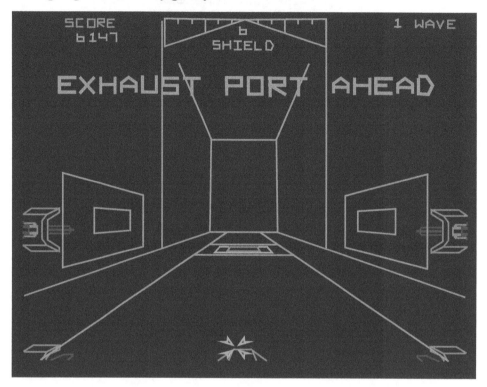

This forces your leaders to focus. You can't have it all. And Spotify didn't start here. Their first version of the bet list had sixty-five initiatives that they thought needed doing. Not ten. And it's a credit to the leaders that they whittled the list down to the size they did and said no to a lot of stuff. That's not easy. But that's what leaders do.

Enables Cross-Company Alignment

But what's really amazing about the company bet is how it enables cross-company alignment. I was lucky enough to work on two number-one company bets during my time at Spotify—the Sony Playstation and the Google Chromecast. The way the company rallied around these initiatives, under very tight deadlines, was incredible to see as shown in the figure on page 57.

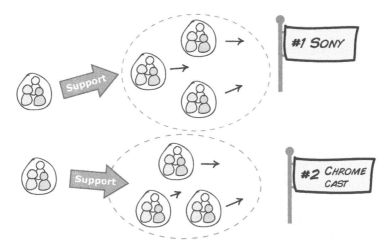

And I have yet to see any other company marshal and deploy resources this effectively. It's how unicorns deliver on really big initiatives fast where most others would fail. And it's how they get the entire company on board behind something while doing everything possible to make it a big success. A wonderful tool for alignment and prioritization.

Tips for Executing

Now I don't want any of this to sound easy. Just because you create a prioritized list and share it with the company doesn't mean everyone is instantly aligned. It still takes a lot of time and effort to make this work—it starts at the top with the leaders, and it needs to be reinforced at every level of the company and communicated clearly on downward.

But after doing a few of these, we learned some things around how to make the execution of company bets go a bit better.

Assign a Full-Time Road Manager

Company bets don't drive themselves. They take a lot of effort, time, and skill. The people we put in charge of company bets were called road managers, and they were the ones responsible for ensuring the bet gets done. They drive the bet.

These are critical full-time roles that take someone with experience to lead, communicate, and coordinate the efforts of multiple teams, not always within the same part of the organization. Google and Facebook call these people product managers. And they can make or break the delivery of a bet. So choose wisely when assigning someone to this role.

Think Beyond Your Part of the Organization

Something our road managers discovered when executing was that just because you're number one in your part of the organization doesn't necessarily mean you're number one in the others. Tech Product and Design (or what we called TPD) was organizationally separate from HR and Legal. So if you need the help of other departments you don't interface regularly with, make sure you have a mechanism for coordinating and sharing priorities with them. The company bet list was our way to ensure we got on their radar.

Come Up with a Communication Plan

When collaborating with multiple teams over different locations, you need clear and open communication channels throughout the organization. It's easy for people not co-located directly where the work is being done to feel excluded or like second-class citizens. To fix this we had a very structured, frequent, proactive communication plan. Weekly demos, physical space, clear meeting cadences, along with explicit communication guidelines like regular check-ins, asynchronous updates, email groups, and announce-lists.

Keeping everyone in the loop and feeling like they are included is very important.

Integrate Early

If you're working on something that involves integrating multiple partners and systems, integrate early and often. Nothing really works the first time you hook things up, and we realized how hard it can be to get different systems working internally (much less with outside partners over whom we have no control). So connect things as early as possible end-to-end. And resolve whatever issues come up then and there.

Stagger the Big Ones

Something we learned the hard way at Spotify was the cost of running two big bets at the same time. Our resources got really stretched. People weren't happy. Overtime was put in. And even though one bet is higher priority than the other, that doesn't mean number two isn't important, and it can be hard to choose.

What we learned from this was that we sometimes needed to stagger certain types of work so as to not put too much stress on the system all at once. Else things will break and no one will be happy.

The Counter-Intuitive Bet

There's another kind of bet we never talk about in the enterprise. It's something called the *counter-intuitive bet*. And it's the kind around which companies are formed and new industries get built.

Counter-intuitive bets are bets that initially no one believes, but in hindsight look brilliant and obvious. Who in their right mind would ever pay $7 for a cup of coffee? Who is going to want to pay money to sleep on my couch?

Company	Counter-Intuitive Bet
Netflix	Mail order DVDs / Streaming
Airbnb	Rent my couch
Twitter	140 chars of text
Starbucks	$7 for a cup of coffee
Spotify	Convenience over piracy

In 2006 no one believed people would rather pay a monthly fee for access to all the world's music instead of downloading it illegally for free. Spotify was founded on this counter-intuitive bet of convenience over piracy. And that bet has certainly paid off for Spotify and the music industry.

Unicorns love these kinds of bets because these are the bold ideas that can make or break a company while keeping them ahead of the competition. It's how they innovate and stay ahead—until the rest of the world wakes up and realizes what is now glaringly obvious.

Q&A

> HOW DO SQUADS TRADE OFF WORKING ON A BET VERUS WORKING ON THEIR MISSION ?

When squads are creating their work for the upcoming quarter, they first look to see if they can align their mission work with any upcoming bets. If they can, they do. If for whatever reason there are no bets they can currently line up against, they are then free to go back and continue working on their mission.

This is how companies like Spotify and Amazon enable two levels of strategy and planning to happen concurrently.

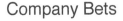

Company Bets

Two Levels of Strategic Planning

Squad Missions

Squads have their missions—they own that. But the company has their higher-level strategy and initiatives too. These are much bigger, requiring more coordination, capital, and planning. And like a laser they focus the company—which is why they can only do a few at a time.

Just to be clear, squads are still the ultimate deciders of where they should be spending their time. That autonomy is still there. The bets and Dibbs are there to help squads out and to make sure they are helping out the rest of the company and not simply suboptimizing for themselves.

But at its heart, the company bet is a communication and collaboration tool. It's how tech companies like Spotify rally the troops around big opportunities, swarm them with everything they've got, and then return to business as usual until the next big thing comes along.

Make a Bet

Unicorns disrupt and execute by making big counter-intuitive bets. Here we learned that company bets are a powerful tool for scaling work across the organization.

To work well, they require road managers to drive and strong communication plans to keep everyone abreast and in sync. They are one way in which tech companies swarm big problems, ensure the most important stuff gets done first, while simultaneously giving squads the latitude and autonomy to continue with day-to-day work.

Next up, let's take a look at what working at one of these tech companies actually feels like and see why day-to-day work there feels so different.

FOOD FOR THOUGHT

How does your company set priorities today?

_____

_____

_____

	Yes	No
Does everyone know what those priorities are?	☐	☐

What are your company's top three priorities
for the upcoming quarter?

#1 _____

#2 _____

#3 _____

How do these get communicated out?

_____

_____

_____

What is stopping your teams from collaborating as one today?

_____

_____

_____

CHAPTER 6

Working At a Tech Lead Company

Working at a tech company feels different. And no small part of that is due to how they are led. In the next two chapters, we're going to look beyond the beanbags, lattes, and ping-pong tables and get into what working at a tech lead company looks and feels like through the eyes of someone doing the work.

In this chapter we're going to focus on some different ways tech companies lead, as well as some of the management practices we don't typically see in the enterprise. Then in the next chapter on productivity, we'll shift gears and look at some of the concrete things tech companies invest in to go even faster.

The goal of these next two chapters is awareness. I want you to get a sense about what working at one of these tech companies feels like—not so you can blindly copy, but more so you can see how they are led, the type of culture they try to create, and why people enjoy working there so much.

The World Is Flat

In June 1957, at the Clift Hotel in San Francisco, Robert Noyce and seven other of the country's most talented scientists and engineers couldn't take it anymore. Their company's founder, William Shockley, was proving unbearable to work with. Since winning the Nobel Prize in physics for inventing the transistor, Shockley's ego and management style started to eclipse his genius.

He became rigid. Authoritarian. Impossible to please. He started blaming others for bad decisions he had made, while simultaneously taking credit for other people's work. He was intolerant of new ideas and views that differed from his own. He offered no way for people to share in the rewards of what they made beyond their base salary. And through his bad management style, he alienated just about every smart, enterprising scientist and engineer in the company.

So on that fateful morning, this ragtag group, later to be known as the Traitorous Eight, left Shockley Semiconductor and started their own company. And thus Silicon Valley's very first startup was born.

Fairchild Semiconductor quickly became the poster child for a new way of working—one based on an entirely different set of principles that reflect how many tech companies, particularly in Silicon Valley, work today.

Flat hierarchies. Casual meritocratic workplaces where what you did mattered way more than your title or role. Where you were encouraged to share new ideas, and it was perfectly OK to go up to the CEO and say why you disagree.

Spotify had this informal casualness about it. Many people didn't start till later in the day. Others, like me, preferred to come in early. But that's entirely the point. So long as you got your work done, when you came in didn't matter.

And that's the first difference. Way more autonomy. Way more freedom. But also a lot more responsibility. Which is why when you first join one of these tech companies, it can feel rather strange—because for the first time in your career, no one is looking over your shoulder telling you directly what to do.

I'm Not Going to Tell You What to Do

Perhaps one of the biggest shifts in management style at a lot of these tech companies is that for the first time in your career, you aren't told exactly what to do. Instead, you're encouraged to think and figure things out for yourself.

I saw this firsthand one day when the heads of two squads came to my boss with a problem—they couldn't agree on who should take ownership of a recently abandoned product.

Periodically, when tribes reorganize, old squads get disbanded and new ones form. And sometimes who owns what can get a little confusing.

In this case there was no owner for an existing product. The old squad went away. And the two new squads couldn't agree on who should take the old product over. So they asked the tribe lead, my boss, to decide for them. Except he wouldn't.

After hearing both sides of the argument, my boss replied. "That's a real interesting problem you have there. Let me know what you decide."

Tech companies, at least Spotify, prefer it when people make decisions for themselves. They don't like telling people directly what to do. And as a North American, coming from a more command-and-control style structure, this can seem really strange at first. It's so much easier and faster, when you have one decider, to simply tell people what to do!

The World's First Startup

Fairchild Semiconductor became the role model for a new way of working. For example, Fairchild was one of the first companies to offer direct ownership to employees in the form of options and shares. Robert Noyce, one of the eight founders, was also famous for rejecting the plush corner office and instead sitting in a plain old regular cubicle like everyone else.

This isn't how most traditional companies feel—where executives get reserved parking, only vice presidents go for offsites, and you wouldn't dare tell the CEO what you really think. Which is why working at a startup or tech company feels so different. Very flat. Very meritocratic. No special privileges. We're all in this together.

From this single company, a trillion-dollar industry emerged right in the heart of California whose impact is still being felt to this day through its descendants—or what are otherwise sometimes referred to as the Fairchildren.

Signetics	Ameico	Applied Materials
AMD	Intel	Apple
VLSI	Oracle	Sun
SanDisk	Nvidia	Ebay
Google	Yahoo	Facebook
Tesla	LinkedIn	Cadence
WhatsApp	Linear	Maxim
Instagram	Pinterest	Snapchat

www.computerhistory.org/atchm/fairchild-and-the-fairchildren/

Except for one thing. When you tell people what to do, they don't own it. You do. Which is why, at a lot of tech companies, you don't have managers wandering the halls, micromanaging and making decisions for teams. They much prefer setting the stage and laying out the principles, and then letting the teams work things out for themselves.

And that's why my boss wasn't going to make this decision for them. "Come to me if you lack information, context, or have bigger-picture questions. But this is something you need to work out among yourselves. I'm not going to tell you what to do."

A Different Attitude Toward Money

From the outside, it looks like tech companies spend money like drunken sailors. Free lunches, endless snacks, fruit and coffee, offsites include everyone, good computers. It's all there.

Scratch the surface a little deeper, however, and you'll find there's method to the madness. Tech companies spend money on things traditional companies won't because it makes them go faster.

I remember sitting across from my same boss one day asking if it was OK if I ordered dinner for the team who were staying late to hit a tight deadline. Whose permission did I need? And what forms did I need to fill out? All that kind of stuff.

"Don't worry," he said. "If the team needs dinner, just buy it. In fact, if you can spend money to make the team go faster, do it!"

That caught me off guard. Never before, in my professional career, had anyone told me to spend money in the name of speed. But that's exactly what tech companies do.

- Need a new mouse? Order it.

- Need to be in Gothenburg to better coordinate work with another team? Why are you still here? Go!

- Know a book that would help the team write better software? Buy three and share it with others.

Well-funded tech companies who have found product market fit are in a race. And if they can deploy capital to win that race, they will. That's why they don't sweat the small stuff. They want their teams to go as fast as they can. And if giving you some discretionary spending will help the team go faster, they'll do it. Because remember, tech companies value speed and learning above all things—which is a big reason for why they trust.

Don't You Trust Me?

Trust   No trust

After joining a tech company or startup, it quickly becomes clear how little you were really trusted at the traditional company where you used to work.

For example, at big traditional companies these restrictions are not uncommon:

- You have no administrative access to your computer.

- Certain websites are blocked.

- You are denied access to social media.

- There's no amount of discretionary spending.

- You're forced to run productivity-killing virus scanners while doing development.

- You must change your password three times a day.

OK, I'm exaggerating on the last one, but you get my point. Traditional companies don't trust their employees, and it really slows everything down in countless ways.

Compare this with big tech companies:

- Developers have full access to their machines.
- All teams have access to production.
- There are no restrictions on which websites you can visit.
- You are free to use any social media you like.
- You are free to install any software you want.
- You are encouraged to book your own travel.
- You are free to order and buy pretty much anything you need.

In other words, we trust you. We trust you not to waste money. We trust you not to abuse this privilege. And if showing you the company's financials and other sensitive information will help you do your job better, we trust you with that information too. Because at unicorns, information is defaulted to open.

All Information Is Defaulted to Open

My first week at Spotify was in some ways overwhelming because never before had I been exposed to so much data—company financials, the latest subscriber numbers, key company metrics, status reports from just about every project in flight. All this information, while fascinating, was like drinking fine wine from a fire hose. It was almost too much.

What I didn't realize at the time was that this is another core tenet of how these tech companies operate. At Spotify all information was defaulted to open. This reinforces a core belief many others tech companies have:

PEOPLE MAKE BETTER DECISIONS WHEN GIVEN ACCESS TO ALL THE DATA.

With the exception of things like salary and compensation (though we debated making those open too), pretty much all information at tech companies is defaulted to open. Meaning if there's a piece of information you need to help you make a decision, you get it.

Defaulting information to open does three things:

1. It leads to better decision-making.
2. It's a huge signal of trust.
3. It makes everything easy and faster.

As information is pushed further down, teams aren't making false assumptions about how users are using the product, or about where potential opportunities for innovation or improvement lie. They can see the information and make product decisions for themselves.

And by making potentially sensitive financial and performance numbers open, tech companies are sending a huge signal of trust. They trust that you aren't going to abuse this data. They trust you aren't going to do anything malicious. And when given their trust, you can't help but want to reciprocate that trust back.

And companies that trust their employees simply go faster, as their attitude is why would we hire someone we didn't trust?

Apple's Secrets

One big exception to this rule of thumb around defaulting information to open is Apple. For years, Apple has been one of the most secretive companies in the world—and for good reason. Their products are copied. Their product launches are legendary. And you can't surprise the masses if they know what's coming. There'd be no famous Steve Jobs "Just one more thing"–like moments.

But that's changing. With Steve gone, and Tim Cook now at the helm, Apple is slowly opening up in ways it never did before.

Apple engineers still can't blog or write about work the way engineers at Google or Facebook can. But, now, for the first time in years, you are seeing Apple engineers attend conferences, write papers, and even contribute to open source.

Netflix, Facebook, Google, and Spotify engineers all regularly visit and talk to one another about how they're building product, doing automated testing, and all the heavy lifting required to build those amazing products. Apple not so much.

Slowly this is changing—partly because their employees are demanding it, and partly because even Apple is realizing that there's a lot to be gained by at least defaulting some information to open and engaging with others in the tech community at large.

Can I Help You?

Tech companies, and the teams within them, really support each other. If you walked up to just about any Spotify squad and asked them for help, not only would they help you with your immediate problem, they'd sit down with you, work through whatever problem you had, and do their best to make sure you walked away feeling like a happy customer. That's because the attitude these teams have is we're all on the same team. And you, if you've got a problem, I've got a problem. So I had better help you out.

Sounds simple, but when you compare it to the way most traditional enterprise teams work, you quickly see how damaging all those projects, budgets, and perverse short-term incentives really are.

For example, one question a lot of teams in traditional companies get when engaging another team for help is: "What's your charge code?"

What they are asking you for is whose budget they should charge their time against to help you out. No charge code. No help.

That's what help looks like within a lot of large enterprise companies—charge codes, service tickets, and perverse short-term incentives that prevent the right things from getting done.

Tech companies collaborate circles around the incumbents when it comes to cooperating, because their incentives are aligned. By getting rid of the project, assigning teams missions, and aligning through bets, they create a much simpler fluid model of work—one that is way less concerned about whose project it is and where to charge time and money, and instead more focused on solving the customer's problems and getting the work done.

Let Tech Lead

This chapter was short, but hopefully it gives you a bit of a sense of how these kinds of tech companies work and a few of the different ways tech companies are lead:

- Way more autonomy
- Way more freedom
- A lot of responsibility
- No one telling you directly what to do
- All information defaulted to open

Another way in which tech companies lead differently is that they invest in all the things we know we should invest in in the enterprise but never seem to—either because they are deemed too expensive, or we just do not have the time.

In the next chapter on productivity, we'll look at some of the investments tech companies make in the name of productivity and why certain things that are notoriously hard in traditional companies (like building and shipping new product) are a breeze and non-events for these tech unicorns.

CHAPTER 7

Invest In Productivity

One thing tech companies are very good at is investing in things that enable them to go fast—specifically productivity. Things we have to fight ridiculously hard for in the enterprise (like investing in productivity and infrastructure), tech companies simply do.

In this chapter, we're going to stop and see what these investments are and why they enable tech companies to move so fast.

Create Productivity Squads

Productivity squads are teams whose mission is to make other engineering teams go faster.

Just think about that for a minute. What teams do you have in your organization whose sole purpose is to make the lives of people shipping and building product easier. Tech companies are full of them.

These productivity, or infrastructure, squads help others:

- Automate builds
- Work on continuous integration (CI) infrastructure
- Build A/B testing frameworks
- Create production deployment/monitoring tools
- Build automated testing frameworks
- Construct infrastructure to easily add new features
- Host training sessions
- Transform and migrate data
- Iterate and learn faster

This is all the stuff enterprise development teams know would enable them to go ten times faster but never seem to be given the space or time to do. Making smart investments in infrastructure and productivity is how tech companies deploy new software with ease, know what's going on in production at a glance, and effortlessly crank out new products and features.

But more than that, instead of being gatekeepers and policing how teams deploy these services into production, these teams create self-serve models where other squads are able to help themselves.

Adopt Self-Service Models

Productivity teams don't stand between squads and production. Instead they enable them and provide the means for teams to help themselves.

At a traditional company, for example, if I wanted to spin up a new database instance for my project, I would probably need to fill out some forms, answer a whole bunch of questions, seek someone's permission, and then sit and wait a couple weeks for the request to work its way through the system.

Tech companies don't think like that. If you need a database, continuous integration server, or an instance of something in the cloud, simply go to the wiki page, follow the instructions, and set it up yourself. Go!

Tech companies work hard to remove any friction between teams and delivery. And this manifests itself in other ways too.

Instead of ordering keyboards, mice, and USB connectors every time someone needs one, they simply stock a small store with all these items on standby, and you come and help yourself. Instead of vending machines for candy, they have vending machines for basic equipment people generally need. Simply tap your employee badge and go.

Of course, the unwritten rule is to only take what you need and not to be wasteful. But by avoiding the form filling, permission seeking, and red tape most traditional companies seem to enjoy setting up for employees, tech companies don't sweat the small stuff. And everyone moves faster because of it.

Host Hack Weeks

Hack week is a week Spotify set aside, twice a year, where engineers could work on whatever they want. This is one of the vehicles tech companies use to try new ideas out and let people innovate. The bet here is that by letting people work on their passion projects, new product ideas and features will come out. Google famously pioneered this idea with it 20% time rule (where you were allowed to dedicated 20% of your work time to whatever side project you wanted). This led to the development of Gmail, Google Maps, and AdSense.

You could work by yourself. Team up with others. And you were generally free to work on whatever you wanted. The only rule was that at the end of the week, you had to get up on stage and show people how you spent your time.

This created a nice sense of accountability as well as putting an onus on shipping. You were strongly encouraged to ship something—something you could demo.

So during the week people would work really hard, often putting in more time they they normally would at work. And then when Friday came, we'd all gather around the main stage, and people would then demo their hacks. Some of them were amazing.

You would see things like these:

- Collaborative playlists

- New ways of visualizing music

- Dashboards for reporting flaky tests

- Maps for meeting rooms (meeting rooms were sometimes hard to find at Spotify)

- Cow bells that played to the best of music by analyzing the frequency of drums (more CowBell!)

- Reduced compilation times on really large projects

While only a few of the hacks ever turned directly into product, what hack days accomplished was something bigger:

- Brought the company together
- Enabled people to collaborate with those they didn't usually get to work with
- Helped create and foster strong bonds across the company
- Let people showcase their unique talents and creativity
- Served as a vehicle for learning
- Was a heck of a lot of fun

Whether it's hack days, hack weeks, or 20% time, tech companies give their people time and space to explore because of the energy it brings. Sometimes it results in new products and innovation. But more than that, tech companies want people to bring that passion and energy to work everyday when they come in. And if the price of tapping that passion is giving them a few days a year to work on whatever they want, that's a price they're willing to pay.

Leverage Highly Technical Product Owners

Product owners (or product managers as Google likes to call them) are the visionaries or customers behind the products tech companies build. To agile folks, these would normally be referred to as customers—or the people from business who know the requirements of the systems to be built.

But in tech companies, being a product owner or manager is a much bigger role. Not only do product managers steer product, they also set expectations with others in the the company, handle external relationships with vendors, and push to make sure the right things get done.

They're also highly technical. Many are former engineers with a deep understanding of technology and design, and with a passion for learning. What this means is tech companies typically don't suffer from that artificial divide between technology and business.

This gives them a huge advantage in execution. Not only can they talk to what the product needs to do, they can translate that more easily into terms engineers building the product understand.

Have Higher Expectations Around Quality

Tech companies have a higher expectation when it comes to quality, and this manifests itself primarily in two different ways.

First, code quality at tech companies tends to be much higher. Code I regularly see in the enterprise would never pass a code review at Google or Facebook. It's not just the quality of the engineers. It's the expectation of the work.

Poor design decisions that are tolerated in the name of budget and schedule are simply not accepted at tech companies. They understand the implications that come from cutting corners, so they simply don't accept crap work. They send it back. They tell the engineers to try again. Any only when it's good enough do the changes get accepted and merged into master (the repository holding the code for the product or service).

The other way quality manifests itself at these tech companies is in their platforms and systems. Because tech companies are founded and led by engineers, they don't have to justify and fight for projects to improve the quality of their systems. They simply do them.

That's why Spotify spent two years shoring up their systems to support global music streaming and Amazon spent over a year migrating from their monolith into a more decentralized web service–based architecture. It didn't offer any immediate benefit. But they knew to get where they wanted to go, it just needed to be done. So they did it.

No New Features for Two Years

In July 2011 Spotify had a problem. It had just launched in the United States, it had a big partnership with Facebook, but its systems were falling over. All those users, streaming all the music, was simply too much for Spotify's internal systems. It's couldn't keep up.

It's at that point that Daniel Ek, Spotify's CEO, went to the board and delivered a message no CEO ever wants to give. He basically said Spotify was not going to add any new features to the product for the next year. Instead they were going to work on internal scaling and infrastructure. The board agreed. He ended up taking two.

Not every traditional company needs to spend two years shoring up their infrastructure, but these are the kinds of bets and investments unicorns make. If it's important, they do it. And it's a big part of why their systems work, why they are able to move so fast, and why their customers love their products.

A Brief History of Spotify: Gustav Söderström

www.youtube.com/watch?v=jTM7ZCKEUGM

As an engineer, this affects you in two ways.

1. You create higher-quality work because it is expected

This comes as a relief because now that the excuse of budget and schedule are taken away, you have the time to build things right. These systems need to work, and they need to work well. It's not that there isn't pressure to ship. It's more that there's pressure to build it right. And because the long-term incentives line up, people end up caring more and the result is higher-quality work.

2. You go faster

Because the whole company is putting this level of care into their work, and poor design decisions in the name of budget and schedule aren't being tolerated, a virtuous cycle of feedback and speed begins to form.

You start trusting and relying on other teams for their work. They are relying on and trusting you for yours. And the whole ship moves faster.

Utilize Internal Open Source

Another important practice tech companies employee when building software is this model of internal open source. Internal open source means anyone in the company can check out anyone else's code, at any point in time.

They can propose changes. Fix bugs. Make suggestions. Just like the open source model used in the real world.

Internal open source is handy for several reasons.

1. You are never blocked

If you need a bug fixed, or the team maintaining that portion of the product doesn't have time to help you out, you can check out code, create the PR (pull request), and make the changes yourself.

2. Fewer bottle necks

Because anyone can work on the codebase at any point in time, multiple streams of work happen simultaneously. This removes the team as the bottle neck and lets other teams contribute simultaneously, all independent of one another.

3. Guided collaboration

Internal open source isn't a free-for-all. The changes you make have to be vetted by the owners of the system. But this is good. It enables you to do the work that needs to be done. And it also ensures the work gets implemented in a consistent and well-designed way. This strikes the right balance between enabling anyone to make a change and ensuring the change gets made right.

Continuously Improve at All Levels

Spotify was pretty good with trusting and empowering squads with a great deal of autonomy. But one thing they didn't leave to chance was insisting that squads strive to continuously improve. The mantra at Spotify was that you will continuously improve (whether you like it or not).

Some of this was structured—agile coaches regularly did health checks and retrospectives, and management continually met and thought about ways to help make squads better.

But what was most impressive was how Spotify did retrospectives for the really big company bets. When a company bet finished, every team that participated in the bet was included in a company-wide retro, and the results of those retros were then sent to all the teams and senior management.

And these weren't always pretty. Real feedback came out. Real suggestions on how to improve. And we admitted when mistakes were made, and miscommunications happened. I don't know if other tech companies do this the way Spotify does. I know Google and Pixar do a lot of post mortems, and Spotify will also do these for service outages or specific events.

But that mantra of continuous improvement is definitely baked into the DNA—and goes right to the heart of the company.

You're Just Gold-Plating

I was once on an enterprise project where the technical lead suggested a design that would fix the problem quickly but lead to a whole bunch of misunderstanding and confusion for developers later in the product. When the other engineer and I pushed back, he said, "You guys are just gold-plating."

This wasn't a term of endearment. What he was basically saying was you guys are over-engineering this, and you should just accept my design because we can build it fast and it will work.

This tech lead was a strong, enterprise developer. But he had also been conditioned to tilt heavily toward budget and schedule and not think long-term about the implications of the design. This happens all the time in enterprises. Bad decisions get made in the name of deadlines and budgets. Tech companies aren't immune to this either. They just have a much higher threshold around what is acceptable and encourage engineers to build it right in the first place.

Utilize Feature Flags

Tech companies have had to get very good at releasing. And two practices that are a big part of their releasing playbooks are feature flags and release trains.

Feature flags (aka feature toggles) are software switches that let teams turn certain features in their software ON or OFF in production. Why would anyone want to turn off a feature? Two reasons—integrating unfinished work and running experiments.

Managing unfinished work has always been a pain in software. You either keep it outside of the core product (and integrate it later when it's done) or you integrate it, but then have this awkward state where the feature is included but not yet really working.

Feature flags solve both these problems by letting teams merge their unfinished work into the codebase, by hiding it behind a feature flag, so development can continue without impacting the end customer.

```
ON ( ) OFF
if onboardingEnabled {
  showOnboarding()
} else {
  showLogin()
}
```

Feature Flag
A way of hiding unfinished work
or dynamically turning
a feature ON or OFF in
software in production.

This also simplifies the integration process and minimizes the number of bugs that often come with delaying the merging until later. And as we'll see in the next chapter, Chapter 8, Learn with Data, on page 81, feature flags are also how tech companies run countless experiments in their products by simultaneously deploying multiple versions and then seeing how customers use them.

But where feature flags really get powerful is when you combine them with release trains.

Ship with Release Trains

Release trains are batches of completed features you regularly ship at predefined intervals. You can ship daily. Every two weeks. Or by the minute, if you like. But the idea is to continuously ship whatever features are done, and then immediately start preparing for the next train to leave the station after that as shown in the figure on page 79.

Release Trains

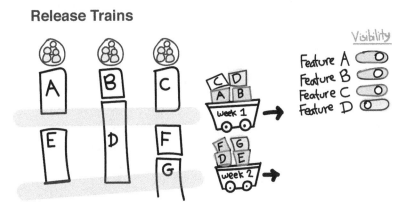

This simple act of continuous releasing does two very important things. One, it removes the stress of trying to cram features in at the last minute to meet some deadline. And two, it lets teams continually make small improvements to the product in smaller batches—which are easier to test and debug.

And when you combine the release train with the feature flag, you have a really nice system for continuously shipping new features, including unfinished work, from a single codebase—even from multiple teams spread across the company (this is how Spotify ships the iOS and Android apps, along with their desktop application).

Enterprise teams traditionally have never needed feature flags or release trains because they've never had to run experiments (though some do use feature flags for hiding unfinished work). You simply build the product once, ship it, and then move on to the next project. No iteration required.

But if you want to compete with tech companies on longer-lived products, ones that you are committed to making better, you'll want to get into the habit of adding feature flags and release trains to your release process. Not only are they essential for iterating, and running experiments, they will enable you to react more quickly, fix bugs faster, and improve your overall customer experience and design.

Make Tech First Class

We covered a lot of ground in these last two chapters, but hopefully that gave you a bit more of a feeling for how these tech companies think about delivery, as well as some of the investments they continually make in the name of productivity and execution.

In a nutshell, tech companies treat tech as a first-class citizen, and they wield it very effectively as a means to go faster:

- They make deliberate investments in productivity.
- They trust and empower their teams.
- They don't cut corners on tech—they treat their infrastructure as a first-class citizen.

There's one more area that tech companies excel in, and that is the collection and use of data. Turn the page to see how tech companies regularly use data to make product decisions better, and how you can gain insight into how customers are using your product.

CHAPTER 8

Learn with Data

In this chapter on data, you're going to see the lengths tech companies go to leverage data as a tool for making their products better. Not only will you see how data is collected and stored, you'll learn about a new role tech companies use to help gather and process all this data, as well as how instrumenting your product can lead to better product decisions.

Learning how to leverage data will give you new insights for features, help you and your team innovate, and give you a leg up on the competition when it comes to product and execution.

Data Everywhere

When you first join a tech company, one of the first things you quickly get an appreciation for is just how big a role data plays in product creation. It's everywhere.

It starts at the top, with key metrics of the company. For a music streaming service like Spotify, that means tracking things like monthly active users (MAU), daily sign-ups, and number of paying premium users. Every time we had a town hall, the discussion revolved around these numbers, where they were trending, and why.

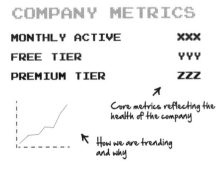

COMPANY METRICS

MONTHLY ACTIVE	XXX
FREE TIER	YYY
PREMIUM TIER	ZZZ

Core metrics reflecting the health of the company

How we are trending and why

Then you get the big company bets. These are the big rocks the company hopes will materially move the needle commercially for the company. How many sign-ups did we get as a result of that partnership? Are we seeing good numbers as a result of launching in Japan. Big rocks. Hopefully, big numbers.

And then near the bottom you have all the metrics each tribe and squad keeps for their particular mission. What tracks are popular for morning commutes? How many people monthly are streaming music on speakers? How is our retention trending on TVs?

Now traditionally, in bespoke enterprise application development, we typically don't track metrics like this because there's never been any need to. Our customers are in-house. They don't really have any choice regarding whether they use our software or not. And once the software is shipped, the project is over. There's nothing to track.

Outward-facing product development is different. Here, your customer isn't in-house. No one is telling you directly what to do. You need to go out there yourself and figure out what's working for your customers.

Which is why the first thing any tech company does from the beginning when shipping product is instrument and collect data on how people are using it.

Instrument Your Product

Instrumenting your product means capturing those events in your applications that give you insight into what your customers are doing.

For example, if we were building a photo sharing application, it would be good if we knew how people were moving through the app when they were using it.

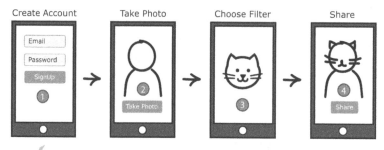

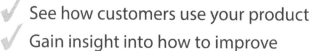

✓ See how customers use your product
✓ Gain insight into how to improve

If the goal is to share, not only could we track how many times people successfully shared, we could also track and see where people are getting stuck along the way.

The other thing that's handy to do is capture key tap events. For example, say as a squad we thought we could increase our company's MAUs (monthly active users) by giving our users the ability to create collaborative playlists when starting a road trip.

Instead of just building this feature, shipping it, and hoping for the best, we could capture key events people performed when creating collaborative playlists and then use that data to draw insight.

Capture key tap events

Group Chat		Choose title		Add songs	
Search ●		Road trip ●		Search ●	
▶ Tom Sawyer	→	Next Cancel	→	▶ Derezzed +	
▶ YYZ		● ●		▶ Owner +	
▶ Analog Kid				▶ SOS +	
Create ●				Share ●	

Maybe the create group playlist button isn't displayed predominantly enough on the screen. Maybe people didn't realize Search initially displayed their recently played songs. Or maybe it wasn't clear what songs were in the playlist and what songs weren't.

Whatever the question, we can't answer it until we know how customers are using our product. So instrumenting gives us that insight. It lets us iterate, improve, and test.

Now, the real, interesting question is what to do with this data once we have it. For example, what if we come up with some design alternatives around how customers could share better, but were unsure as to which one was the best?

Believe it or not, there's a way to answer this question by simultaneously trying both designs out. And tech companies do this all the time with something called an A/B test.

Experiment with A/B Tests

A/B tests are experiments tech companies run in product to see which designs work better.

Say, for example, we think that the reason no one is sharing our newly created collaborative playlist is because once users add a whole bunch of songs, the Share button gets pushed down to the bottom of the page and no one sees it unless they scroll down. And we're wondering if moving the Share button up would result in more shares.

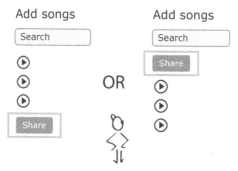

When faced with questions like this, tech companies don't just pick one. They try both.

A/B Test   A way of running experiments on product

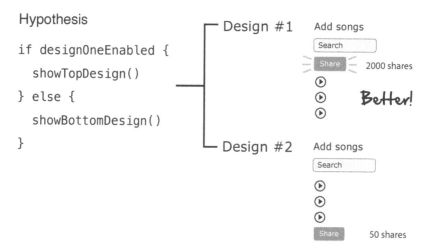

By moving the Share button to the top of the page and seeing how many users click Share there (as opposed to it sitting at the bottom), tech companies can try both designs out before fully committing to one of them. And by continually iterating and running little experiments like these, they can quickly calibrate around what works.

This is called an A/B testing. And tech companies run experiments like these all the time when building product. If the test shows that one design results in more shares than another—that's good! It gives them a clue that they're on the right track. If it doesn't, that's OK too. At least they know before fully committing and shipping.

The mechanics of the A/B test and the feature flag are almost the same. The difference with the A/B test is you need an extra mechanism to decide what portion of users you want to direct to your new design. Usually you start with something small (say 1, 3, or 5%). Then once you are confident you've worked most of the kinks out, you steadily ramp it up until you're happy and confident it can replace what was there previously.

Typical examples of A/B tests would include things like these:

- Number of search results to display
- Length of a link
- Gravity factor in a video game
- Call to action (CTA) text and copy on buttons
- Headlines and copy for marketing

 ## A/B tests are just a tool

A/B tests are powerful, but you've got to be careful how you use them. They don't replace thinking. And you need a large amount of data before they are statistically relevant.

For example, just because one A/B-tested design resulted in a higher conversion number than another doesn't necessarily mean it's better. There might have been a marketing campaign driving more traffic to that portion of your app while the experiment was running. Or by turning off one feature but simultaneously turning on another, you might have had two tests cross paths, which affected the user in an unanticipated way.

Also, for A/B testing to work effectively as a full-on experiment, you need a lot of users and data. Most companies don't have the number of users Google, Amazon, and Facebook have. So for them, A/B testing isn't going to be as meaningful or significant.

Instead, what usually works better is going out, talking to ten customers, and asking them what they love or hate about your product.

A/B testing can also affect your work. You'll need to prioritize experiments just like stories in your backlog. And you're going to need people to help you make sense of all the data you're collecting and come up with the right experiments to run.

For these kinds of tasks, you're going to want the help of a data scientist.

Would You Recommend This Product to a Friend?

One metric tech companies track religiously when building product is their product's NPS, or net promoter score. NPS is a measure of the likeliness you or someone else would recommend your product to a friend.

It's literally one question: "Would you recommend this product or service to a friend." You then get them to answer this question on a scale from 0 to 10 (10 being the highest).

- 9–10 are called promoters
- 0–6 are known as detractors
- 7–8 results are thrown out

So if you have an NPS score of 80%, that means 88% percent of people gave your product a 9 or a 10, 8% of people gave your product a 0-6, and 12% gave it a 7 or 8.

Anything above 50% is really good. This number can get negative (which is where a lot of product starts). But it's a universal measure tech companies use and track to figure out how much people are loving or hating their product.

Source: Y Combinator, David Rusenko—How to Find Product Market Fit

www.youtube.com/watch?time_continue=692&v=0LNQxT9LvM0

Enter the Data Scientist

Data scientists are mathematicians and engineers who help people make sense of their data. With the sheer amount of data and computing power companies have today at their disposal, there's a need for experts who can collect, process, clean, filter, and then infer sight on large amounts of data. And because data processing has become so cheap, everyone can leverage these tools and insights—not just big companies.

At Spotify, data scientists would help teams:

- Decide what metrics to collect
- Format and clean data from different formats
- Come up with naming conventions for tagging and collection
- Create hypotheses and tests
- Determine which results were statistically significant

- Perform exploratory data analysis
- Set up reports, summaries, and dashboards

Sometimes this was one person. Sometimes two (it could be a full-time job just getting the data into a state where it could be analyzed).

But the key point here is that data processing is no longer something exclusive for senior managers at large companies. Tech companies give this power to their small autonomous teams, and then wield it with great effect when building product. And data, along with rigorous analysis, is very much at the heart of how these tech companies operate.

Ever Heard of a Machine That Can Learn?

Unless you've been hiding under a rock, you've no doubt heard a new term enter the tech lexicon—machine learning or ML. Machine learning is what enables Netflix to suggest movies, Spotify to recommend songs, and Google's autonomous vehicles to drive themselves.

Basically, huge amounts of data are thrown into computer-training algorithms, and the machines learn how to classify certain types of information and then use that in applications. It requires massive amounts of data, huge amounts of computing power, and will one day shortly be available to you.

Machine learning is just one of many examples of tech companies leveraging data they have collected over the years into new products and services that would have been impossible only a few years ago. And it's also why you are seeing such an increase in demand for people with math and statistical analysis skills.

Leverage Data

Don't let the shortness of this chapter fool you. Data is a big part of how tech companies operate. Step one is instrumenting your product so you know what your users are doing. Step two is then analyzing that data with the help of someone like a data scientist.

In the next chapter, we're going to look at how tech companies use culture to create better workplaces. And we'll see that culture is the one thing no upcoming unicorn leaves to chance.

CHAPTER 9

Reinforce Through Culture

Culture is one of those things tech companies used to let form on its own. Not anymore. It plays too important a role to be left to chance—which is why so many tech companies invest directly in culture and use it to reinforce the good, while putting a stop to the bad.

In this chapter we'll focus on what makes company culture good, as well as core beliefs some tech companies apply when shaping it. This will give you an idea of what tech companies value in new hires, as well as the expectations and behaviors they look for in leaders and managers working there.

By the end of this chapter you'll know why culture is so important, why tech companies don't leave it to chance, and you'll have ideas for defining and building your own.

Different Companies Have Different Cultures

Tech company culture is hard to explain, because while there are certainly common traits that describe how tech companies generally work (flat hierarchies, small empowered and trusted teams), even among tech companies the nuances of each can be quite different.

	Design
Google	Engineering
	Shipping product
amazon	Customer first
	Music
NETFLIX	Sports team
PIXAR	Story telling

Take Apple, for example. Apple is arguably one of the most innovative, successful tech companies in the world. And it proudly stands at the crossroads of the arts and science. Yet it's also one of the most secretive companies in the Valley. Here, information is not defaulted to open.

Google's mission is to organize the world's information, while hopefully doing no evil along the way. To do that, Google has had to tackle some of the world's most challenging technical problems. Their culture is very much focused on solving hard-core computer engineering and science problems, using many of the computer science fundamentals we're taught in school.

Amazon wants to be the world's store. But they stress frugality in how they operate (they want all savings to be passed directly onto the customer, much like Sam Walton did with Walmart). They also focus maniacally on the customer—which is why Amazon often works backward from the customer experience.

And while many companies profess wanting work to feel like a family, Netflix has taken the opposite approach and unapologetically defines itself more like a sports team. When you come to Netflix, know that you are playing a role. As soon as that role is no longer required, you're going to be traded or let go.

All these companies empower and trust their employees in similar ways, yet they all have very distinct and different cultures. So what does good culture look like?

In this next section, I'd like to share with you what Spotify culture felt like, along with why I feel it was so effective. We'll then look at some core beliefs, along with some examples of how those beliefs get turned into action.

Spotify Culture

Describing a company's culture is tough because it often fails to capture the spirit and nuance that you only see in the day-to-day. To address that, we're going to look at Spotify culture in three different ways.

First, we're going to look at what Spotify culture feels like from the point of view of a manager and engineer. Here we'll talk more in generalities, discuss what good culture feels like, along with some examples of how culture affects people's lives and careers.

Second, we'll then get more concrete and go over some core beliefs Spotify feels are important to reinforce in the workplace and expectations it has for its people day-to-day.

Reinforcing Culture at Apple

Apple reinforces its unique approach to design and product in several unusual ways. For example, this is the letter all new employees are greeted with on their first day of work.

First Day Letter

There's work and there's your life's work. The kind of work that has your fingerprints all over it. The kind of work that you'd never compromise on. That you'd sacrifice a weekend for. You can do that kind of work at Apple. People don't come here to play it safe. They come here to swim in the deep end.

They want their work to add up to something.

Something big. Something that couldn't happen anywhere else.

Welcome to Apple.

Then they present you with pictures like this, demonstrating Apple's approach when it comes to product and design. This Picasso shows how few lines it takes to draw a bull, reinforcing Apple's mantra that simplicity is the ultimate form of sophistication.

Apple and others are very deliberate about the kinds of culture they want to create. It isn't something they simply leave to chance, as it has too much bearing on their success and work.

Then third, I'll share with you some stories demonstrating culture in action— because action is the ultimate manifestation of culture. Otherwise, it's just words.

But let's start with how it feels.

How Does Good Culture Feel?

Feelings about culture are hard to articulate. So let me start by sharing what working at Spotify felt like:

- We believe in you.
- You can believe and trust in others.
- We're all in this together.

- Everyone is here to help.
- You don't need to be afraid.
- We've got your back.
- What do you need?
- We're going to be open and honest with you.
- Respect others.
- We trust you.
- You are empowered.
- Go for it!

The big thing about Spotify is empowerment, trust, safety, and team. At Spotify you never felt like you were alone. You never felt like you weren't supported. And the company was always there to support you and your team in whatever it is you were doing.

Let's start with the team. Spotify puts a ton of effort into building good teams. They want teams to be collaborative, cohesive, fun, and to work well together, because of the core belief that good product comes from good teams. And when you're a part of a team, you're never alone. So you never had the feeling that it was all on you. You had a great support network with your management and your team.

Safety was the other pillar of Spotify culture. You never felt threatened, or scared, or were told to stay in a box and only do one thing. Quite the opposite. Spotify often encouraged you to leave your comfort zone, try new things out, and see how far you could go.

For example, I originally joined Spotify as a technical agile coach. That meant it was my job to go around and help teams with technical practices, and hopefully have some kind of positive effect when it came to building quality product and software.

There was just one problem. After about a year in, I felt like I wasn't getting through to the teams I was coaching. One way I thought I could be way more effective would be working directly with teams, contributing and leading by example as an engineer.

So I talked to my boss, asked him if it was OK if I joined a team full-time as an engineer and tried to bring about change from within. He wholeheartedly supported me. And after a three-month trial, which worked out for both sides, I left my role as technical coach and formally switched to being an engineer.

Spotify didn't have to do that. They could have said: "Thank's, but no thanks, Jonathan. We prefer you right where you are as a coach—not an engineer."

But they didn't. They encouraged me to follow my passion. They entrusted me to do what I felt was the right thing to do. And they supported me every step of the way.

And that's what good culture feels like. It's safe. It's empowering. It's liberating.

Core Beliefs

So that's what good culture feels like. But how do you describe something like that in words? To capture that spirit, Spotify created a set of core beliefs around people and teams, as well as engineering. Let's go over those now—starting with teams.

Beliefs About Teams

Spotify believes the following when it comes to teams.

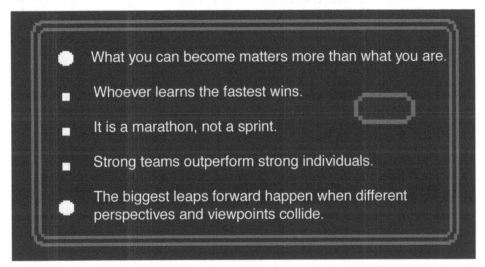

- What you can become matters more than what you are.
- Whoever learns the fastest wins.
- It is a marathon, not a sprint.
- Strong teams outperform strong individuals.
- The biggest leaps forward happen when different perspectives and viewpoints collide.

What you can become matters more than what you are is how Spotify hires. When you apply for a role at a tech company, they're looking for two things. What can you do today, along with what you can do tomorrow.

With this phrase, Spotify is setting the expectation that while you have a role to play today, what we are really excited for is what you are going to be able to do with us in the future. Remember, these tech companies invest a lot in you, and they want you to stick around for a long time. As an employee, this is empowering because it signals a wide open future, beyond what you see in front of you today. So you're encouraged to keep your eyes and ears open, learn new things, and never feel like you have to be stuck in a rut. There are lots of problems out there needing solving, and we see you being a big part of that.

Whoever learns the fastest wins goes to the heart of how Spotify and tech companies tilt when it comes to execution—speed. Everything they do is about speed and learning. Tech companies don't have better people than traditional companies. They simply empower and trust them more. They also aren't doing this because they are inherently nice. They do this because it produces better results —which is why tech companies trust and empower so much. They're trying to move as quickly as possible, learning as much as they can along the way.

It's a marathon, not a sprint is a reminder to all that we're in this for the long haul. So pace really matters. Don't burn yourself out out. Don't cut corners. We're in this for the long haul. Do the right thing.

Strong teams outperform strong individuals. This is an interesting one. What Spotify is saying here is that we value team members who work well together over rock stars who are complete jerks. Not every tech company feels this way. Google, for example, has a reputation of loving rock stars and will put up with a lot of bad behavior if they think it's worth it. Not Spotify. Here Spotify is signaling which way they lean on this topic by making it explicit. We believe in the team over the individual.

The biggest leaps happen with different perspectives is about diversity. Above all else, Spotify values diversity. Spotify started out like most tech companies do—a small group of nerdy young white guys who had a counter-intuitive bet on how to change the world of music. But while making that bet a reality, they quickly realized that they didn't have the world's perspective on how to build a global product. And that if they wanted to build something that would appeal to millions, they were going to need some different perspectives on how to do it.

So those are some beliefs about people and teams. And through leadership and management, Spotify would beat the drum on these loudly when hiring, building teams, and doing one-on-ones, and really remind everyone what good behavior looked like and what we believed when it came to people.

Let's now look at some beliefs around engineering.

Beliefs About Engineering

Spotify believes the following when it comes to engineering:

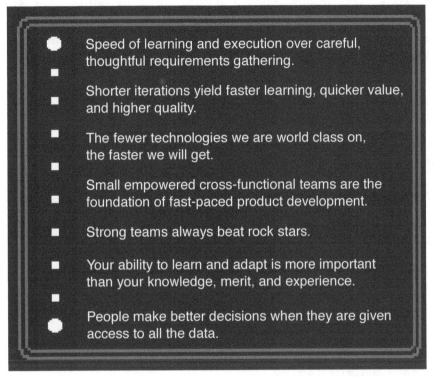

Do some of these sound familiar? Some of these beliefs have their roots in the agile world, while others are direct reflections of what was already covered in beliefs about teams.

Speed of learning over thoughtful requirements gathering and *shorter iterations cycles* are the foundation of agile engineering. We know we can't get all the requirements up front—so don't bother. And we'll learn faster the more times we try. These beliefs make that explicit.

The fewer technologies we are world class on is a counterbalance to unbridled team autonomy. Yes, you can choose how you want to build your product, but we're not going to support 10,000 different languages and technologies. We've settled on these few. Pick from these core ones and go.

Small empowered teams over rock stars we already covered. Spotify favors the team. *Your ability to learn* is a reminder that we don't care so much about your past—we're more interested in your future.

And *people make better decisions when given access to all the data* is the belief that causes all information to be defaulted to open.

These core beliefs around people and engineering are but one way Spotify tries to communicate and reinforce culture within the company. These come up in town halls, one-on-ones with managers, and often in day-to-day decision-making, where it may not always be clear which is the best way to go.

But as good as core beliefs like this are, they alone are not enough. What really makes culture stick is action—action on behalf of the people, action on behalf of the leaders, action on behalf of the CEO.

In this next section, we're going to take a look at culture in action, and see why actions always speak louder than words.

Want to Work at Amazon?

I once had the opportunity to interview for an engineering position at Amazon. While part of it was technical, an even bigger part of it was focused on culture. Here's what Amazon looks for in the people it hires.

Amazon Principles

- Customer Obsession
- Ownership
- Invent and Simplify
- Are Right, A Lot
- Learn and Be Curious
- Hire and Develop the Best
- Insist on the Highest Standards
- Think Big
- Bias for Action
- Frugality
- Earn Trust
- Dive Deep
- Have Backbone; Disagree and Commit
- Deliver Results

These aren't just idle words like the ones you normally see decorating other places of work. Amazon really stresses these from day one. And if you can't demonstrate customer obsession, ownership of problem, or times when you have pushed or insisted on higher standards, they won't hire you—no matter how good you are. Culture is that important to them, and it's also the best defense for maintaining and preserving it.

www.amazon.jobs/en/principles

Action Speaks Louder Than Words

To really make culture work, it needs to be backed up by actions. So in this section, I would like to quickly share with you a few stories that exemplify good culture, along with the corresponding effect it has on the workplace.

I Need Your Help

One day, while sitting at my desk, I saw an email come out from Daniel Ek, our CEO. In the email Daniel explained some of the challenges we were going to face that year. What the current competitive landscape looked like. And then he did something I had never seen any other CEO do. He asked for help.

Daniel came out and basically said this was his first time leading something this big (remember, he was only 28 at the time). And that he was going to need my and everyone else's help if we were going to take on the incumbents and forever change the way music is enjoyed by people around the world.

This email was incredible on two levels. One, I had never seen a CEO be that vulnerable or that honest with employees. But if he can be vulnerable, maybe I can too? Maybe I don't need to pretend I have all the answers. Maybe it's OK to ask others for help even though I'm a senior engineer and everyone is looking to me for guidance.

That email showed more leadership than just about any other act I'd seen at any of the countless companies I had worked at before and was way more powerful than any poster on a wall. Because companies follow their leaders. And Daniel set the stage right there.

I Broke It

One day, a colleague of mine accidentally broke a major system responsible for enabling all music streaming on a particular very popular third-party device. Though he didn't know it at the time, he had accidentally pushed the testing configuration into prod, thereby breaking production.

After some digging, and realizing that he had caused the error, he sent an email to the entire tribe describing what the problem was, how it occurred, and apologizing. He was a new hire. And he felt really bad.

The response from my boss was classic. Instead of coming down on the person, and demanding changes to how we release changes into production, he basically said:

"Don't worry about it. These things happen. Breaking prod is a kind of badge of honor. You aren't the first. You certainly won't be the last. And the fact you were able to do this speaks more to deficiencies in our systems—not your abilities as an engineer or new hire."

This response was perfect. Not only was our leader signalling that mistakes were going to happen. He was signalling that they were OK—and that it was part of the game. And the answer isn't less autonomy and more rules. It's we trust you. We got your back. Get out there and try again.

We Got This

I remember being on a team once that had a hugely important deadline with a major music company. And if we didn't ship by a certain date, we were all going to die. At least that's how it felt.

I raised the fact that we were severely behind schedule, weren't likely to make the date, and sat back to see how management was going to react. What happened next stunned me. Instead of sounding the alarm, calling code red, and demanding action, the program leader calmly looked up and said:

"Well, the team is responsible for this delivery. They'll reach out if they are in trouble. We trust the team to do it."

This was not the reaction I was expecting. I just told them that the number one bet in the company was severely behind schedule, and they were telling me to sit down and relax.

In the end, the team did make it. I was proven completely wrong. And while there were a few weekends and bumps along the way, the team did it. But by not rushing in and trying to solve all the team's problems, management reinforced the sanctity of the team and their trust in their ability to get the job done.

This took a lot of courage, trust, and faith in the team. Most organizations wouldn't have done that—which is why teams are such a big part of the Spotify culture and form the very core of how they deliver.

Who's the Boss

I once sat down with the program leader for the number one company bet we had going at the time in Spotify and asked one of my favorite project manager questions: "Who's the boss."

This is a technique I had used with great success on past projects to cut to the chase and quickly figure out who the real decider was on projects with multiple stakeholders all wanting different things. I asked her point blank and she looked taken aback.

"What do you mean who's the boss? There is no boss. The team will decide."

"OK," I said. "But what if marketing wants to do X, and engineering thinks we should do Y. Who will decide whether we do X or Y?"

Again she says, "The team will decide."

"What if the team can't decide."

"Then it will come up to the leaders of the team, and as a group we will decide if the team can't. But it should never come to us. The team, with the stakeholders, will work things out. There is no boss."

What I had experienced here was my first taste of Swedish culture (Spotify is a Swedish-based company). Unlike North America, where we put a premium on top-down decision-makers, Sweden values a more bottom up consensus-building approach to decision-making—and that my style of management wouldn't fly here.

What this leader was demonstrating through action was reinforcing the Spotify culture in me—by letting me know that Spotify is a consensus-building culture, where we try not to promote a one-leader mentality, and again reinforcing the trust and empowerment of the team-based culture.

Once I realized that, things got a lot easier. No longer did I feel responsible for making all the decisions. Instead, I realized it was my job to help teams make decisions for themselves, using all my experience and insight to help avoid any potential pitfalls along the way.

We Will Not Rush This

Where things really get interesting is when you bring Swedish culture to North America. I once got my wrist slapped by a Swedish agile coach for trying to speed up some decision-making in a big meeting involving various heads of product, design, engineering, and sales.

I suggested that before we reconvene next, the heads of various departments get together, come up with a plan, and then return and share it with the rest of us after. To me this sounded like a pretty reasonable ask, and lots of North American heads were looking at me nodding in agreement.

"I say no, and am playing the company building-consensus card," said the agile coach dramatically as he stood up and played an imaginary card on the table. "We do not short-circuit decision-making here. We must all come to a consensus. As painful as this seems, we will continue this way, as long as it takes, until we are all in agreement."

This agile coach wasn't being pedantic. He was defending the consensus-building culture of Spotify in San Francisco, where the Swedish way of doing things wasn't quite as strong. While facilitating, he was playing the role of cultural ambassador. And while it didn't necessarily feel good at the time, he was right.

He made us all sit in the room, hammer out our differences, and come together in a way I had never seen at that particular office before. It took a strong leader to go against the grain and do that. But that's what leaders do.

They preserve culture and values, even when it feels uncomfortable. Because the more you let it slide, the harder it becomes to bring back—which is why Spotify reinforces its culture so vigorously, and goes to great lengths to keep it alive and well in the workplace.

Swedishness

As I've mentioned, Spotify is a Swedish-based company. Founded in 2006 in Stockholm, Sweden, Spotify has grown to be one of those rare non–North American unicorns with offices now in over fifty-eight countries around the world. And while Spotify competes now with the likes of Apple, Amazon, and Google, it has its own unique brand and culture.

In this section, I'd like to share with you what working for a Swedish-based company looks like, how its culture is slightly different from what we are used to in North America, and the impact that has in the workplace.

Consensus Building

Team-based consensus-driven approaches to work and problem solving are how Swedes like to work—which is why agile software delivery comes naturally to Swedes. They were already working that way.

Swedes are natural team builders, and they are suspicious of people and bosses who come in and start telling them what to do. For this reason Spotify and other Swedish companies favor team-based approaches to solving problems and prefer it when teams figure things out for themselves. It's also why the Swedes don't view the role of boss the same way we do in North America.

Your Boss Isn't Your Boss

Just to be clear, from a practical point of view, your boss is your boss in Sweden. They set your salary. They have a say in your career. And from the outside, for all intents and purposes, they look like a regular North American–style boss.

But when you watch how Swedish managers manage, they operate in a very different way. For one thing, the boss is there to help you. Swedish bosses don't lord over you the way North American bosses do. Instead they show up and try to help.

A one-on-one with a Swedish boss typically goes something like this:

- How are you doing?
- Everything OK?
- You getting everything you need?
- What do you think we could be doing better?
- Anything I can help with?
- I am here if you need me.

Servant-leadership is a real thing over there. And your boss is there to help. And while they do sometimes need to make tough decisions, handle HR issues, and do typical boss stuff, they much prefer it if you come in self-motivated, ready to work, and don't need to be told what to do.

Good Mood in the Workplace

Swedes are really big on everyone getting along in the workplace. They even have a word for it—*bra stämning*. And one tool Swedes use in the workplace to help people get along is this Swedish institution known as the *fika*.

Fika is a team-based coffee break where everyone gets together and has a coffee and a bun. Fika has been a core part of Swedish society for many years, and harks back to the industrial age where people needed a break from working in the factories and would assemble to take a pause.

Everyone attends fika (to not do so is a cultural faux pas). And while you are free to discuss whatever you want, sensitive topics like politics or Norway's continued dominance in cross-country skiing are usually avoided.

Fika is instead seen as an opportunity to get together, know your co-workers, share interests, and bond. The idea here is that teams who bond together work together. And working together is easier if you know your co-workers.

Work-Life Balance—Lagom

Swedes have a word that to them is almost a way of life—*lagom*. Lagom means not too much. Not too little. Just right.

They apply it to everything. Work. Life. Play. Vacations. Candy. You name it. If you're wondering how much of something is enough, the Swedish answer is lagom.

Swedes don't put in as many hours as we do in North America. Five weeks holiday is the law over there, and the entire country shuts down over summer—which makes life interesting for those in the company not working in Sweden.

But despite having to compete with some of the largest, most powerful tech companies in the world, Spotify has found a way to do it without putting in the crazy hours we expect from tech companies in Silicon Valley.

Managers at Spotify get concerned when employees work too much. Often, they tell them to go home if they're staying too late. And it goes back to that core belief. We're in a marathon. Not a sprint. And the result is a much happier, healthier lifestyle for the company and its people.

Listen More Than Talk

Swedes aren't big talkers. They prefer to listen. Which means sometimes you need to work a bit more to ensure everyone's opinion is heard. When you're in a meeting, the proper way to come to a decision is to go around the room, get everyone's opinion, and discuss the best way forward collectively as a team. This prevents loud, overbearing personalities from dominating and ensures every voice is heard.

This is how Swedes like to build consensus. And while this can initially be frustrating for non-Swedes who are used to faster go-go decision-making, the Swedes would rather move more slowly, ensure everyone is heard, and then once consensus is reached, quickly move as one.

The Law of Jante

Jante's Law is an informal code of conduct in Nordic countries describing how one should behave in Nordic society. The Law of Jante goes like this:

- You're not to think you are anything special.
- You're not to think you are as good as we are.
- You're not to think you are smarter than we are.
- You're not to imagine yourself better than we are.
- You're not to think you know more than we do.
- You're not to think you are more important than we are.
- You're not to think you are good at anything.
- You're not to laugh at us.
- You're not to think anyone cares about you.
- You're not to think you can teach us anything.

These rules, captured by Aksel Sandemose in 1933, were an attempt to portray the condescending attitude toward individuality or personal success, which he thought had been a core part of Nordic psyche for centuries.

I never felt this while working at Spotify. And to be honest, I believe many Swedes struggle a little with this feeling of "not going for it"—which is why some of Sweden's best and brightest go abroad to places like America, where individuality and exceptionalism are more accepted and the norm.

But I mention it because it captures several characteristics deeply rooted in Swedish society, like not boasting and not displaying outward appearances of wealth. And it explains why Sweden's richest citizens still take public transit. They don't feel like they are any better than the rest of us.

OK. With that, let's now wrap things up, try to take everything we've covered in the book so far, and tie it all together into one grand unifying theory that explains why the tech unicorns disrupt, and what makes them so successful.

Culture Matters

Unicorns are deliberate about culture. They don't leave it to chance. They invest in it. They cultivate it. And they leverage it when building product.

And while every company will have its own distinct unique take on culture, empowerment and trust are at the heart of most. This is what enables them to move quickly while giving people the opportunity to do their best work. Good culture doesn't just enable good product. It's a requirement tool for finding the best talent. And unicorns understand very well how creative, smart people like to work.

In the next chapter, we're going to wrap up by taking a look at what concrete steps we can start taking to level the playing field with these unicorns today, along with the other longer-term changes required to compete in the future.

CHAPTER 10

Leveling Up—From There to Here

So now that we know what these unicorns do, how do we take all of this advice and put it into practice? That's the subject of this final chapter, as here we will look at some ideas on where to begin, what first steps companies can take, and how to start taking all these ideas and applying them to your place of work.

Let's start by looking at something most traditional companies have forgotten. Their purpose.

Drive with Purpose

The first thing traditional companies can do to get people excited about work is remind people why they are working there in the first place. In other words, remind them of the company's purpose.

Startups, at least initially, don't have the luxury of attracting people with money. So they can't attract talent with big fat paychecks. What they do have in abundance, however, is purpose.

Whether it's saving the planet with electric vehicles, colonizing Mars, or just finding cheaper insurance, all startups begin with a purpose. And they use it with great effect to motivate, attract, and retain talent because, initially, that's all they've got.

But startups do not have a monopoly on purpose. Traditional companies have purpose too! They have just forgotten how to use it, and many would benefit from reminding themselves why the founders started the company in the first place.

Traditional companies need to rediscover their reason for being and remind people why the work they are doing matters. Because once they do that, the why behind a lot of things becomes easier and the path forward clearer.

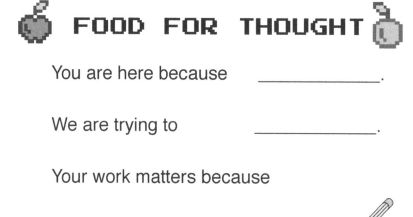

FOOD FOR THOUGHT

You are here because _____.

We are trying to _____.

Your work matters because

_____.

Do You Want to Sell Sugared Water for the Rest of Your Life?

Perhaps the most famous example of a startup selling purpose was Steve Jobs' recruitment of John Sculley for the role of CEO at Apple in 1983.

Apple needed a new CEO. And the thinking was it would be good if it was someone who was really good at marketing. And at that time, John Scully of Pepsi was seen as the best.

The problem was Scully didn't really want to join Apple. Why leave Pepsi, a company he had helped build over the last eighteen years, to join what was then seen as a risky startup from California that might not even be around in five years?

But Jobs was determined—he wasn't going to take no for an answer. So he went out to see Scully, one last time, looked him in the eye and said:

"Do you want to spend the rest of your life selling sugared water, or do you want a chance to change the world?"

John knew at that moment Steve had him. He left Pepsi that year and joined Apple as its new CEO.

Think Strategic—Act Local

Once your teams are armed with purpose, have leadership set the high-level goals. Make this your bet list.

Top 3 Things
We need to do this quarter

1. _____

2. _____

3. _____

Your bet list doesn't have to be company-wide. You can start at a much smaller level—your department for example. Simply have the hard discussions, prioritize with management the biggest, most important things that need to be done. Then act local.

Give these big rocks to your small, empowered, mission-led teams, get out of the way, and let them own it.

Turn This Ship Around

One refrain I hear a lot from traditional companies when it comes to super-empowered teams is that it all sounds great in theory, but it only really works for startups.

That's usually when I recommend they head out and buy a copy of *Turn This Ship Around*. In his remarkable book, David Marquet describes the organizational transformation he and his crew went through on the USS Santa Fe, one of the worst-performing nuclear subs in the U.S. Pacific fleet, and how they transformed it into one of the best. His big secret—Captain Marquet never gave a direct order.

Working primarily through intent, Captain David described the mission, what they needed to get done, and then left it up to his officers and the crew to execute and figure out how to get there.

It's a remarkable story of how a U.S. Navy captain changed the attitude and structure of one of the most extreme, traditional, command-and-control style workplaces in the world, into an open, innovative, empowered place of work.

If the U.S. Navy can do it, so can you.

This last part is important. You want your teams to start taking the initiative, coming up with their own solutions and solving their own problems. This is going to affect the way you work in more ways than one. First, it's going to be unpredictable (something traditional companies typically don't like). Second, it's going to affect how your company budgets—which means changing your budgeting model.

Fund Teams, Not Projects

I know, I know. No one wants to think about budgeting, but it's important. It drives a lot of the function, and dysfunction, we see in companies today.

Traditional companies have a very defined set way in how they allocate capital for future work. And no matter how successful tech companies are, very little is likely to change in how traditional enterprises budget.

But by funding teams instead of projects, you can get rid of a lot of the drama, dysfunction, and waste that comes with budgets and projects—and instead focus on the work and the mission. It would work something like this.

Pick a core part of your business that is super-important—something you want to keep improving and iterating on long-term no matter what. Then instead of doing all the work in the form of one or many projects, fund a permanent team and let them work on it long-term instead.

This will give you all the benefits described in Chapter 2, Give Purpose with Missions, on page 13. But it will also make the core systems of your business first class—which you are going to need if you want to innovate and compete.

Make Tech First Class

Until traditional companies make tech a first-class citizen in the company, they're going to struggle to compete with the very startups they're trying to stay ahead of.

There's no way that Netflix should have a better sign-up experience than every cable company in North America—but they do. And it's not because Netflix knows the customer better. It's because Netflix's underlying technology for signing new customers up, collecting payment, and getting them watching TV is seamless—not to mention a pretty compelling product.

Tech companies invest in tech because they know the advantage this brings them in execution. Yes, incumbents have every advantage in terms of wealth, capital, resources, knowledge, and experience about the business.

But when it comes to execution and leveraging technology, every advantage goes to the tech companies—because they invest in their core systems, fix root-cause problems, and don't put up with long-term hacks, bugs, and workarounds. Tech companies execute fast because all their systems work together.

Of course, tech companies struggle just like the rest of us when they initially bootstrap these systems up. The difference is they don't stop. They continuously reinvest, make things better, and eventually start to move very fast.

Trying to compete with these startups using a project-based approach to delivery isn't even a fair fight. Yes, traditional companies are sometimes saddled with legacy systems. And yes, the technology changes and things move fast.

But until traditional companies realize that their ability to provide new products and services is intrinsically tied to the quality of the underlying IT services as well as the organizational structure supporting them, competing with tech companies in terms of speed and quality is going to be tough.

Act More Like a Startup

Everyone wants their teams to act more like a startup. The problem, however, is very few people have ever worked at startups, or even know what that means.

Acting more like a startup means the following:

- Admitting, at least initially, that you don't yet know exactly what your customer wants

- Having the determination to find out

- Putting a premium on learning and discovery

- Shipping quickly, getting rapid feedback from real customers, and continuously iterating on product until you perfectly meet the customer needs

It also means dropping all the wasteful budgets and projects. Shifting the focus back onto solving the customer's problem. And focusing instead 100% on doing the work.

And, of course, the vehicle for doing all this is small, empowered, highly trusted teams.

Embrace Small Autonomous Teams

The evidence is clear—small empowered autonomous teams are the way to go. Too many decisions, too much initiative, too much love and care are required to build great products, and this almost never comes from the top down. The only way to build great product is from the bottom up.

If you want your people to own it, you need to give them the authority and trust. Else they are always going to be vegetable choppers. No one is ever going to take initiative and lead. And you'll continue to be stuck with product that comes in on time and budget but that no one really cares about or loves.

Copy with Context

Looking to others for inspiration can be good, and you can learn a lot from studying how these unicorns operate. So I definitely recommend continuing to study how the best companies in the world do it, and trying to glean whatever gems you think will help you and your teams become successful.

Of course, there are no silver bullets. And there are no easy answers to complicated questions—which is why you always need to be careful when trying new ideas, and not simply blindly copy what others have done.

Changing the culture of a company is tough. Reading this book, and hearing how other companies operate, may sound relatively straightforward and easy (it's not rocket science). But it's only when you go and actually do it that you realize how much organizational resistance one can face, and that putting some of these things into action is really hard.

Not every company has a culture of safety. Not every leader is keen to have their department blown up and reorganized. Not all leaders are into this servant-leadership thing. And not every employee necessarily wants to be empowered.

Spotify spent years developing their culture, expectations, support mechanisms, middle management, leadership, and everything else that goes into making Spotify Spotify. There are no shortcuts. You're going to have to do this too.

For those companies who already have a culture built on trust, support, and helping others, this transition is going to be more natural and easy. For others, with fiefdoms and perverse short-term incentives to protect, it's going to be hard.

But there's one big advantage you'll have over those who resist this way of working. Most people in this industry enjoy working this way. And as more and more ideas like this start to take hold in places of work, more and more will come to expect it. Not only is it better for business—it creates better workplaces.

So take these models and ideas. Use them as inspiration for how others are working. But remember to adapt, embrace, and make them your own. While the underlying principles will always hold, implementing them at your place of work will require you to tweak and adapt.

This is a long-winded way of saying context matters. Take these ideas. But make them your own.

Drive—The Surprising Truth About What Motivates Us

In his book *Drive*, Dan Pink points out that it's not money that motivates most people to do their best work. It is instead autonomy, mastery, and purpose. Unicorns are a direct reflection of this, and it explains why so many people love working there and how they produce such great products and results.

Drive explains why people volunteer their free time to work on open source software, why money is such a terrible motivator for innovation, and why our best and brightest are continually attracted to those companies who let them:

- Direct their own work (autonomy)
- Improve in what they are doing (mastery)
- See meaning in what they do (purpose)

It's an excellent book. You can get the gist of it by watching the ten-minute video posted below. But it's a must-read for anyone who is wondering why so many people are drawn to this way of working and what the science is behind why so many corporations struggle when it comes to employee motivation.

https://www.youtube.com/watch?v=u6XAPnuFjJc

Drive: The Surprising Truth About What Motivates Us, Dan Pink

---

Lead by Example

As a leader at your company, know that you are always being watched. If your actions are not consistent with your words, people will heed your actions. Not your words.

- Do you punish those who fail? Or back them up?

- Do you wade in when things are going bad? Or let teams figure things out for themselves?

- Do you trust your teams' estimates? Or do you override them with edicts from above?

- Do you promote people who demonstrate the ideals you speak? Or just those who can ride roughshod over others and get the job done?

To make these ideas stick, you need to promote and support those individuals who can embody the ideals you'd like to see in the workplace. So look for those who support their teams through thick and thin and are always trying to make their teams better, while at the same time leading by example while doing what's right for the company.

Empower and Trust

What this book really comes down to is two words—empowerment and trust. That's it.

What makes these unicorns such great places to work is the amount of empowerment and trust they give people and their teams.

It's what brings out the best in their people. It's why people enjoy coming in to work. And it's how they produce such great results. Empowered, trusted people simply do better work than those who are not. It's what drives people to do their best—because when you're the one calling the shots on your own work, what's the alternative to not giving it your all?

The secret sauce to how these places work is the latitude and empowerment they give these small teams. Because at the end of the day, what they are really doing is taking away the excuses.

Take Away the Excuses

What Spotify did, more than any other company I have ever seen, is take away all excuses.

When you give teams unrealistic project plans, or a nonsensical edict from above, you aren't just giving them bad work. What you are really giving them is excuses.

- It's not my crazy deadline. Its management's.
- It's not my wacky architecture. It's someone else's.
- I wasn't asked. So I didn't say.

When you empower, trust, and give people responsibility, you take away the excuses we all give ourselves when things don't work out. And when we can't blame anyone else but ourselves for how things are going, that changes the dynamic of the work.

- Now they are the ones driving.
- They are the ones calling the shots.
- They are responsible.

It creates a different level of ownership and accountability that you don't typically see in traditional companies. It also creates a sense of pride and quality of work. People really care about their work when they're the ones driving it. It's their baby—which is why you see a level of care, attention to detail, and follow-through in tech companies that you don't in others.

By taking away the excuses, tech companies support teams and try to give them every chance to succeed instead of fail. And when they do fail, they don't assign blame. They reflect, look at ways to improve, and try again.

It's a much better way of working. It delivers far superior results. And it's a heck of a lot of fun.

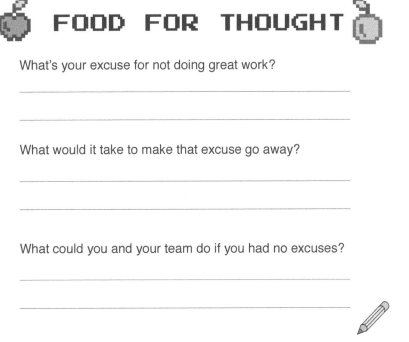

FOOD FOR THOUGHT

What's your excuse for not doing great work?

_____

_____

What would it take to make that excuse go away?

_____

_____

What could you and your team do if you had no excuses?

_____

_____

Final Words

I hope you enjoyed reading this book. I sure enjoyed writing it. There's nothing these unicorns do that you can't. It just takes a different mindset, attitude, and way of looking at work.

The good news is that as more and more people get exposed to this way of working, more and more are seeking it—which is why I am hopeful we'll see a lot more of this startup-style, empowered way of working in traditional workplaces. More people are simply demanding it.

Know that you play a big role wherever you are—and that you can help bring about this change no matter what role you play in your organization. Just keep asking for responsibility. Taking initiative. And as you demonstrate your and your team's ability to deliver, more accountability and trust are going to start coming your way.

I love working this way. I hope you and others will enjoy working this way too. And I wish you every success in building the type of workplace where you can come in, do your best work, be yourself, and go home happy at the end of the day.

Good luck! See you next time.

Jonathan Rasmusson

Index

Thank you!

How did you enjoy this book? Please let us know. Take a moment and email us at support@pragprog.com with your feedback. Tell us your story and you could win free ebooks. Please use the subject line "Book Feedback."

Ready for your next great Pragmatic Bookshelf book? Come on over to https://pragprog.com and use the coupon code BUYANOTHER2020 to save 30% on your next ebook.

Void where prohibited, restricted, or otherwise unwelcome. Do not use ebooks near water. If rash persists, see a doctor. Doesn't apply to *The Pragmatic Programmer* ebook because it's older than the Pragmatic Bookshelf itself. Side effects may include increased knowledge and skill, increased marketability, and deep satisfaction. Increase dosage regularly.

And thank you for your continued support,

Andy Hunt, Publisher

SAVE 30%!
Use coupon code
BUYANOTHER2020

Programming Flutter

Develop your next app with Flutter and deliver native look, feel, and performance on both iOS and Android from a single code base. Bring along your favorite libraries and existing code from Java, Kotlin, Objective-C, and Swift, so you don't have to start over from scratch. Write your next app in one language, and build it for both Android and iOS. Deliver the native look, feel, and performance you and your users expect from an app written with each platform's own tools and languages. Deliver apps fast, doing half the work you were doing before and exploiting powerful new features to speed up development. Write once, run anywhere.

Carmine Zaccagnino
(368 pages) ISBN: 9781680506952. $47.95
https://pragprog.com/book/czflutr

Agile Web Development with Rails 6

Learn Rails the way the Rails core team recommends it, along with the tens of thousands of developers who have used this broad, far-reaching tutorial and reference. If you're new to Rails, you'll get step-by-step guidance. If you're an experienced developer, get the comprehensive, insider information you need for the latest version of Ruby on Rails. The new edition of this award-winning classic is completely updated for Rails 6 and Ruby 2.6, with information on processing email with Action Mailbox and managing rich text with Action Text.

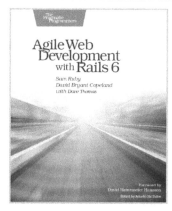

Sam Ruby and David Bryant Copeland
(494 pages) ISBN: 9781680506709. $57.95
https://pragprog.com/book/rails6

Modern Systems Programming with Scala Native

Access the power of bare-metal systems programming with Scala Native, an ahead-of-time Scala compiler. Without the baggage of legacy frameworks and virtual machines, Scala Native lets you re-imagine how your programs interact with your operating system. Compile Scala code down to native machine instructions; seamlessly invoke operating system APIs for low-level networking and IO; control pointers, arrays, and other memory management techniques for extreme performance; and enjoy instant start-up times. Skip the JVM and improve your code performance by getting close to the metal.

Richard Whaling
(260 pages) ISBN: 9781680506228. $45.95
https://pragprog.com/book/rwscala

Fixing Your Scrum

Broken Scrum practices limit your organization's ability to take full advantage of the agility Scrum should bring: The development team isn't cross-functional or self-organizing, the product owner doesn't get value for their investment, and stakeholders and customers are left wondering when something—anything—will get delivered. Learn how experienced Scrum masters balance the demands of these three levels of servant leadership, while removing organizational impediments and helping Scrum teams deliver real-world value. Discover how to visualize your work, resolve impediments, and empower your teams to self-organize and deliver using advanced coaching and facilitation techniques that honor and support the Scrum values and agile principles.

Ryan Ripley and Todd Miller
(240 pages) ISBN: 9781680506976. $45.95
https://pragprog.com/book/rrscrum

The Pragmatic Bookshelf

The Pragmatic Bookshelf features books written by professional developers for professional developers. The titles continue the well-known Pragmatic Programmer style and continue to garner awards and rave reviews. As development gets more and more difficult, the Pragmatic Programmers will be there with more titles and products to help you stay on top of your game.

Visit Us Online

This Book's Home Page
https://pragprog.com/book/jragile
Source code from this book, errata, and other resources. Come give us feedback, too!

Keep Up to Date
https://pragprog.com
Join our announcement mailing list (low volume) or follow us on twitter @pragprog for new titles, sales, coupons, hot tips, and more.

New and Noteworthy
https://pragprog.com/news
Check out the latest pragmatic developments, new titles and other offerings.

Save on the ebook

Save on the ebook versions of this title. Owning the paper version of this book entitles you to purchase the electronic versions at a terrific discount.

PDFs are great for carrying around on your laptop—they are hyperlinked, have color, and are fully searchable. Most titles are also available for the iPhone and iPod touch, Amazon Kindle, and other popular e-book readers.

Buy now at *https://pragprog.com/coupon*

Contact Us

Online Orders:	*https://pragprog.com/catalog*
Customer Service:	*support@pragprog.com*
International Rights:	*translations@pragprog.com*
Academic Use:	*academic@pragprog.com*
Write for Us:	*http://write-for-us.pragprog.com*
Or Call:	+1 800-699-7764

Lightning Source UK Ltd.
Milton Keynes UK
UKHW030239180522
403143UK00002B/6